SIMPLY WINDOWS™
MICROSOFT® WINDOWS™ 3.1

Sarah E. Hutchinson
Stacey C. Sawyer
Glen J. Coulthard

THE IRWIN ADVANTAGE SERIES
FOR COMPUTER EDUCATION
♦
IRWIN

Chicago • Bogotá • Boston • Buenos Aires • Caracas
London • Madrid • Mexico City • Sydney • Toronto

©Richard D. Irwin, Inc., 1995

All rights reserved. No part of this publication may be reproduced, stored in a retrieval system, or transmitted, in any form or by any means, electronic, mechanical, photocopying, recording, or otherwise, without the prior written permission of the publisher.

Printed in the United States of America.

ISBN 0-256-18310-4

Windows is a trademark of Microsoft Corporation

1 2 3 4 5 6 7 8 9 0 ML 1 0 9 8 7 6 5 4

CONTENTS

SESSION 1:
FUNDAMENTALS

Why This Session Is Important   3

What Is Windows?   3
    The Windows Environment   4
    Program Manager   4
    File Manager   4
    Print Manager   5
    Accessory Programs   5
    Task Manager   5
    TrueType Fonts   6
    Multimedia Applications   6
    Windows NT   6

The Windows Advantage   7

Working with Microsoft Windows   8
    How the Mouse Is Used   8
    How the Keyboard Is Used   9

Starting Windows   9

The Guided Tour   11
    Application Window   11
    Document Window   13

Executing Programs and Commands   13
    Menu Bar   14
    Dialog Box   14

Manipulating Windows   16
    Sizing a Window   16
    Moving a Window   18
    Organizing Windows   19
    Selecting Windows   21

Playing Games   21
    Solitaire   21
    Minesweeper   22

Exiting Windows   23

Summary   24

Key Terms   25

Exercises   26
    Short Answer   26
    Hands-On   26

SESSION 2:
WORKING WITH WINDOWS

Why This Session Is Important   31

Program Manager   31
    The StartUp Group   33
    Creating a New Group   33
    Deleting Groups and Program Items   35

Control Panel   36
    Choosing a Color Scheme   37
    Customizing the Desktop   39
    Using a Screen Saver   41
    Choosing a Printer   43

Print Manager   43

Getting Help   44

Summary   47

Key Terms   47

Exercises   48
    Short Answer   48
    Hands-On   48

SESSION 3:
USING WRITE AND OTHER ACCESSORY PROGRAMS

Why This Session Is Important   55

Using Write   55
    Creating a Document   56
    Saving a Document   57
    Opening an Existing Document   58
    Selecting and Editing Text   59
    Formatting Text   61
    Printing a Document   65
    Leaving Write   66

Using Paintbrush   66

Using Other Accessories   70

Multitasking   72

Summary   76

Key Terms   77

Exercises   78
    Short Answer   78
    Hands-On   78

SESSION 4:
MANAGING YOUR WORK

Why This Session Is Important   83

What Is File Management?   83

What Is Disk Management?   84

File- and Disk-Naming Conventions   84

Using File Manager   85
    The Guided Tour   86
        Customizing the Directory Window   88
        Selecting Drives   89
        Selecting Files   89

Managing Files   91
    Customizing the Directory Contents Pane   91
    Working with Multiple Directory Windows   93
    Copying and Moving Files   95
    Deleting Files   97

Managing Disks and Directories   98
    Creating a Directory   99
    Selecting a Directory   101
    Copying and Moving Files to Subdirectories   102
    Removing a Directory   102
    Renaming a Directory   103
    Preparing New Disks   104

Summary   104

Key Terms   106

Exercises   107
    Short Answer   107
    Hands-On   108

USING THIS GUIDE

This tutorial is one in a series of learning guides that lead you through the most popular microcomputer software programs available. Concepts, skills, and procedures are grouped into session topics and are presented in a logical and structured manner. Commands and procedures are introduced using hands-on examples, and you are encouraged to perform the steps along with the guide. Although you may turn directly to a later session, be aware that some sessions require, or at least assume, that you have completed the previous sessions. For maximum benefit, you should also work through the short answer questions and hands-on exercises appearing at the end of each session.

The exercises and examples in this guide use several standard conventions to indicate menu options, keystroke combinations, and command instructions.

MENU INSTRUCTIONS

In Windows, all Menu bar options and pull-down menu commands have an underlined or highlighted letter in each option. When you need to execute a command from the Menu bar—the row of menu choices across the top of the screen—the tutorial's instruction line separates the Menu bar option from the command with a comma. For example, the command for quitting Windows is shown as:

    CHOOSE: File, Exit

This instruction tells you to choose the File option on the Menu bar and then to choose the Exit command from the File pull-down menu. The actual steps for choosing a menu command are discussed later in this guide.

KEYSTROKES AND KEYSTROKE COMBINATIONS

When two keys must be pressed together, the tutorial's instruction line shows the keys joined with a plus (+) sign. For example, you execute a command from the Windows Menu bar by holding down [Alt] and then pressing the key with the underlined or highlighted letter of the desired command.

To illustrate this type of keystroke combination, the following statement shows how to access the File menu option:

PRESS: [Alt]+f

In this instruction, you press the [Alt] key first and then hold it down while you press f. Once both keys have been pressed, they are then immediately released.

COMMAND INSTRUCTIONS

This guide indicates with a special typeface data that you are required to type in yourself. For example:

TYPE: `Income Statement`

When you are required to enter unique information, such as the current date or your name, the instruction appears in italics. The following instruction directs you to type your name in place of the actual words: "your name."

TYPE: *your name*

Instructions that use general directions rather than a specific option or command name appear italicized in the regular typeface.

SELECT: *a different pattern for the chart*

ADVANTAGE DISKETTE

The Advantage Diskette, provided with this guide or by your instructor, contains the files that you use in each session and in the hands-on exercises. This diskette is extremely important for ensuring the success of the guide.

If you are using this guide in a self-study program, we suggest that you make a copy of the Advantage Diskette using the DOS DISKCOPY command. When the guide asks you to insert the Advantage Diskette, you insert and work with the copied diskette instead. By following this procedure, you will be able to work through the guide again at a later date using a fresh copy of the Advantage Diskette. For more information on using the DISKCOPY command, please refer to your DOS manual.

SESSION 1

SIMPLY WINDOWS: FUNDAMENTALS

In the mid-1980s, Bill Gates, the driving force behind Microsoft Corporation, had a vision for changing the way people worked with personal computers. That vision came to fruition with the introduction of Windows, a graphical complement to Microsoft's MS-DOS operating system. In this first session, you are guided on a hands-on tour of Microsoft Windows.

PREVIEW

When you have completed this session, you will be able to:

Explain the advantages of Microsoft Windows.

•

Load Microsoft Windows.

•

Describe the components of the Windows screen.

•

Move, size, maximize, and minimize windows.

•

Automatically arrange windows.

•

Choose commands from the Menu bar and dialog boxes.

•

Exit Microsoft Windows.

Session Outline

Why This Session Is Important
What Is Windows?
    The Windows Environment
    Program Manager
    File Manager
    Print Manager
    Accessory Programs
    Task Manager
    TrueType Fonts
    Multimedia Applications
    Windows NT
The Windows Advantage
Working with Microsoft Windows
    How the Mouse Is Used
    How the Keyboard Is Used
Starting Windows
The Guided Tour
    Application Window
    Document Window
Executing Programs and Commands
    Menu Bar
    Dialog Box
Manipulating Windows
    Sizing a Window
    Moving a Window
    Organizing Windows
    Selecting Windows
Playing Games
    Solitaire
    Minesweeper
Exiting Windows
Summary
    Command Summary
Key Terms
Exercises
    Short Answer
    Hands-On

WHY THIS SESSION IS IMPORTANT

This guide leads you step-by-step through the Microsoft Windows software program. Developed by Microsoft Corporation, Windows makes learning computers easier with its consistent, user-friendly graphical interface. Windows enables users at all levels to take full advantage of today's sophisticated software programs and to work more productively. By the completion of this guide, you will have the fundamental skills for working with application software programs in the Windows environment.

WHAT IS WINDOWS?

Microsoft Windows is an *operating environment* or *shell* that enhances DOS with a **graphical user interface** or GUI (pronounced "goo-ey"). With DOS, you give the computer instructions by typing in commands at a system prompt such as C:\>. Windows, on the other hand, lets you communicate with the computer using a pointing device called a **mouse**. A much faster and easier method than entering commands on the keyboard, you slide the mouse across your desk to move an onscreen arrow over top of pictures or symbols called **icons**. When you have positioned the onscreen arrow correctly, you simply press the mouse button to have the computer execute the desired instruction.

Windows is often referred to incorrectly as an *operating system*. An operating system manages the resources of the computer and its basic input and output operations. DOS is the operating system for the majority of personal computers; other operating systems include OS/2 and Unix. The next Windows version, code-named Chicago, is scheduled for release in late 1994 and combines DOS and Windows into a single product.

Microsoft first announced Windows in 1985. However, the product did not gain widespread commercial success until the release of Windows 3.0 in May 1990. With Windows 3.0, Microsoft enhanced the user interface and memory support and improved the overall performance of the program. Microsoft released Windows 3.1 in the spring of 1992 and the Windows for Workgroups 3.11 Add-On in late 1993. Both versions concentrated on increasing performance and reducing the number of system crashes.

The Windows Environment

Many types of software enable users to perform a wide range of processing tasks—some examples are:

- word processing software for creating documents, such as Microsoft Word (🖉) or WordPerfect (📄),
- spreadsheet software for analyzing numerical data, such as Microsoft Excel (📊) or Lotus 1-2-3 (🔵),
- database software for storing and manipulating information, such as Microsoft Access (🗃), and
- graphics software for creating presentations or designing artwork, such as Microsoft PowerPoint (📽) or CorelDRAW! (🎈).

To satisfy all your computing requirements, you typically use more than one type of software program. Before Windows, learning how to use a variety of programs was difficult because each program had its own set of menus, commands, and procedures. Microsoft Windows makes learning new software programs easier by providing a standardized menu system and user interface for all its applications.

Program Manager

In Microsoft Windows, Program Manager acts as the main menu for the programs on your computer. You organize applications into groups that suit your personal work style and launch applications such as File Manager, Print Manager, and Control Panel. When you close Program Manager, you are also closing Microsoft Windows.

Program Manager is discussed in Session 2 of this guide.

File Manager

Before Windows, most file and disk management tasks were performed from the DOS command line. To copy a file or format a disk, you entered a cryptic DOS command that resembled a line from the "Computer Programmer's Handbook." With File Manager, Windows takes the frustration out of managing your files and disk storage areas.

In particular, File Manager performs the following functions:

- Organizes and manipulates files, directories, and disks
- Copies, moves, renames, and deletes files
- Creates, renames, and removes directories
- Formats, copies, and labels hard disks and floppy diskettes
- Launches your application programs.

In Session 4, you practice managing files and disks using File Manager.

PRINT MANAGER

When you print a document in Windows, the document is sent to an intermediary program called Print Manager. Print Manager increases your productivity by allowing you to send several documents to the printer at the same time while you continue to work in an application program.

Print Manager performs the following functions:

- Stores documents sent to the printer in a print queue
- Manages the priority and order of printing documents
- Pauses, resumes, and deletes print jobs.

Print Manager is discussed in the latter part of Session 2.

ACCESSORY PROGRAMS

Included in the Windows package are several accessory programs, ranging from personal productivity tools to advanced utility programs. For example, Windows provides a basic clock program that enables you to display the current time on the screen while you work with other applications. Windows also provides full-featured programs such as Write, a word processing program, and Paintbrush, a paint program.

Several accessory programs are introduced in Session 3.

TASK MANAGER

Windows is a multitasking environment that allows several programs to be running at the same time. For example, you can run the Windows Clock program, Write word processor, and Paintbrush all at once. You use Task Manager to control the applications that are running in memory and switch from one to another.

TRUETYPE FONTS

One of the more interesting features of Windows is its ability to work with different **typefaces** or styles of print using a **WYSIWYG** (What You See Is What You Get) display. With WYSIWYG, what you see on your screen is what you will get at your printer. Windows standardizes different typefaces for applications and printers using a feature called **TrueType**. (*Note*: Microsoft Windows applications use the terms *typeface* and *font* interchangeably. Traditionally, however, a **font** is defined as all the symbols and characters of a single typeface for a particular point size.)

TrueType allows you to manipulate scalable typefaces to produce onscreen fonts that closely match your printed output. Being scalable, TrueType fonts enable you to select any typeface of almost any size and have Windows immediately display a crisp WYSIWYG image of the typeface onscreen. Windows 3.1 includes 14 TrueType fonts, and you can purchase additional fonts as desired.

MULTIMEDIA APPLICATIONS

Windows enables you to use new and exciting technology, including multimedia applications that incorporate audio tracks, animation, video clips, and photographic images. To access all the special multimedia capabilities of Windows you require special hardware, such as an audio board, CD-ROM, or a personal computing system that meets the Multimedia Personal Computer (MPC) Specification.

WINDOWS NT

Microsoft Windows NT differs significantly from Windows 3.1 in several areas. Windows NT is a full-featured 32-bit operating system, similar to OS/2, and is marketed for high-level computing needs. The minimum system configuration for Windows NT requires an 80386 computer, 8 MB of RAM (Random Access Memory), and a large hard disk (80486 computer with 16 MB of RAM recommended). Windows 3.1, on the other hand, is produced for the average personal computer user and requires a minimum system configuration of an 80286 computer with 1 MB of RAM (80386 computer with 4 MB of RAM recommended). This guide focuses on the capabilities and features of Windows 3.1 and Windows for Workgroups 3.11 only.

THE WINDOWS ADVANTAGE

Windows provides a common environment for your applications with a standardized mouse and keyboard interface. The knowledge you gain from learning one Windows application helps you to learn other Windows applications. Some advantages of working in Windows include these factors:

- *The ability to run more than one application at a time.*
  Windows is a **multitasking** environment whereby more than one application or program may be running at the same time. This feature is especially important for electronic mail, modem, or fax programs that must be running in order to inform you of incoming messages.

- *The ability to copy and move information among applications.*
  Windows provides a program called Clipboard to copy and move information within an application or among applications. Because more than one application can be running at the same time, it is very easy to copy information from a spreadsheet to Clipboard and then paste the information from Clipboard into a document.

- *The ability to link or embed objects from one application into another.*
  The latest products being released for Windows have the ability to integrate applications using a feature called OLE (pronounced "Olé") or Object Linking and Embedding. This feature enables you to embed an object created using one application into another application and facilitates sharing and manipulating information. An object may be a document, worksheet, chart, picture, or even a sound recording.

- *The ability to display on the screen what you will get at the printer.*
  This WYSIWYG feature allows different fonts, borders, and graphics to be displayed on the screen as they would be printed on your printer.

- *The ability to enhance documents with multiple fonts and graphics.*
  In Windows, you can choose from multiple typefaces, font sizes, and graphic images to create various types of documents.

WORKING WITH MICROSOFT WINDOWS

Microsoft Windows is a graphical program. To fully appreciate its functionality, you need to become familiar with using a mouse. Although it is possible to use Windows with only a keyboard, much of the program's basic design revolves around the availability of a mouse.

How the Mouse Is Used

A typical mouse has two or three buttons. You use the left mouse button for selecting the majority of items and commands. In some applications, you can use the right mouse button to access context-sensitive menus. For example, pressing the right mouse button while the onscreen arrow is over text in a Microsoft Word document yields a pop-up menu with editing and formatting commands.

Common mouse actions in Windows are click, double-click, and drag:

- Click — Press down and release the left mouse button quickly. Clicking is used to position the cursor, to select commands, and to choose options from a dialog box.

- Double-Click — Press down and release the left mouse button twice in rapid succession. Double-clicking is often used to select and execute a program or procedure.

- Drag — Press down and hold the left mouse button as you slide the mouse on your desk. The mouse pointer or arrow moves across the screen. When the mouse pointer reaches the desired location, release the mouse button. Dragging is used to move icons or windows or to select text.

You may notice that the mouse pointer changes shape as you move the mouse over different parts of the screen. Each mouse pointer shape has its own purpose and can provide you with important information. As shown in Table 1.1, there are several mouse shapes that may appear in Windows.

Table 1.1	Symbol	Name	Description
Mouse Pointer Shapes	▶	arrow	Used to choose menu items, make selections from dialog boxes, or move windows
	⧖	hourglass	Tells you that Windows is occupied and to wait until it is finished processing
	I	I-beam	Used to modify and edit text and to position the cursor in text boxes
	☞	hand	In the Help window, the hand is used to select topics, jump terms, and definitions

As you proceed through this guide, other mouse shapes will be explained as they appear.

HOW THE KEYBOARD IS USED

Aside from being the primary input device for entering data, the keyboard offers shortcut methods for performing commands and procedures. For example, several menu commands have shortcut key combinations listed to the right of the command in the pull-down menu. Many of these shortcut key combinations are available throughout Windows applications.

STARTING WINDOWS

Because Microsoft Windows requires several megabytes (MB) in storage capacity, this session assumes that you are working on a computer with DOS and Windows installed on your hard disk. In most cases, the hard disk of a personal computer is drive C: and Windows is stored in a directory called \WINDOWS. (*Note*: Your computer's setup may differ without affecting your ability to complete the exercises in this guide.)

Perform the following steps on your computer.

1. Turn on the power switches to the computer and monitor. The C:\> prompt or a menu appears announcing that your computer has successfully loaded DOS. (*Note*: Your computer may automatically load Microsoft Windows when it starts up. If you see the Microsoft Windows logo appear on the screen, move on to the next section.)

2. To start Microsoft Windows from the C:\> prompt:
   TYPE: win
   PRESS: [Enter]
   After a few seconds, the Windows logo appears on the screen followed by the Program Manager window (Figure 1.1). (*Note*: The icons in your Program Manager window may not be exactly the same as in Figure 1.1; the icons represent the programs stored on your hard disk.)

Figure 1.1

The Microsoft Windows Program Manager

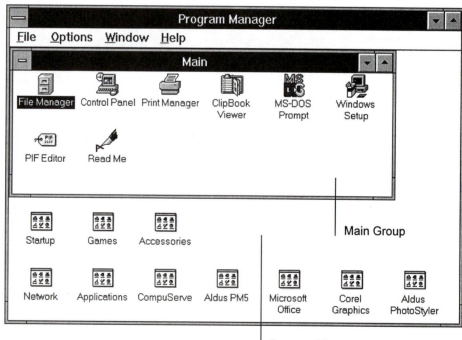

| Quick Reference | TYPE: win |
| Starting Windows | PRESS: [Enter] |

THE GUIDED TOUR

When you first load Windows, Program Manager appears in an application window on the desktop. The Windows **desktop** resembles an ordinary desk in that you have a limited amount of space in which to open and spread out your work. Each application program that you run appears in its own rectangular area on the desktop called an **application window**. In the application window, you create your work in **document windows**.

Inside the Program Manager window, there are several **group icons** and **group windows**. A group window is a special type of document window that contains **program icons**. To launch an application, you open the appropriate group window and then select the application's program icon. If you have just installed Windows on your computer, the Main group window appears in the top left corner and contains general system applications, such as File Manager, Print Manager, and Control Panel.

APPLICATION WINDOW

Application windows, such as Program Manager in Figure 1.2, have the following characteristics: Title bar, Menu bar, Control menu, and Minimize and Maximize buttons. In an application window, you can open multiple document windows simultaneously. Document windows contain the actual work that you create and store on a disk.

Figure 1.2

Application window

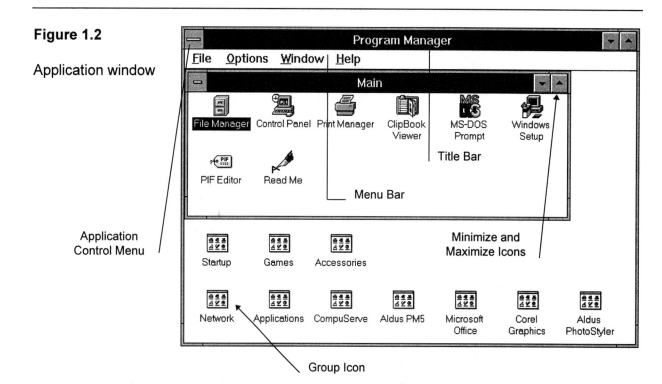

TITLE BAR   The Title bar, located at the top of a window, contains the name of the application or current document. In Figure 1.2, "Program Manager" appears in the application Title bar and "Main" appears in the document or group Title bar. The Title bar also differentiates an active window, which has a darker-colored Title bar, from a nonactive window. Using a mouse, you can move a window by dragging its Title bar.

MENU BAR   The Menu bar appears on the second line from the top in an application window and contains commands for manipulating items in the window. The Menu bar is accessed by holding down the [Alt] key and pressing the underlined letter of the desired command or by clicking on the command using the mouse. When activated, the Menu bar displays a pull-down menu. To leave the Menu bar, press [Esc] twice or click outside the Menu bar.

CONTROL MENU   Every application window and document window has a Control menu that appears as a small horizontal bar in the top left-hand corner. The Control menu is used to manipulate a window using the keyboard. To close an application or document window, select the Close command from the pull-down menu or double-click the Control menu.

MINIMIZE AND MAXIMIZE ICONS   The Minimize and Maximize icons are located in the top right-hand corner of an application or document window. These triangular-shaped icons control the size and display of a window using a mouse. Applications are often minimized from view when they are not currently needed but must remain running. Minimized program icons appear along the bottom row of the desktop.

DOCUMENT WINDOW

Document windows provide the work space for an application. When there is more information available than can appear in the document window at a single time, scroll bars are displayed at the right or bottom borders. You use the scroll bars to move around in a document window by clicking the arrow heads (◄, ►, ▼, and ▲) at either end of a scroll bar or by dragging the "Thumb" or scroll box (▪). Figure 1.3 shows the Control menu, program icons, and Minimize and Maximize icons for the Main group window.

Figure 1.3

Main group or document window

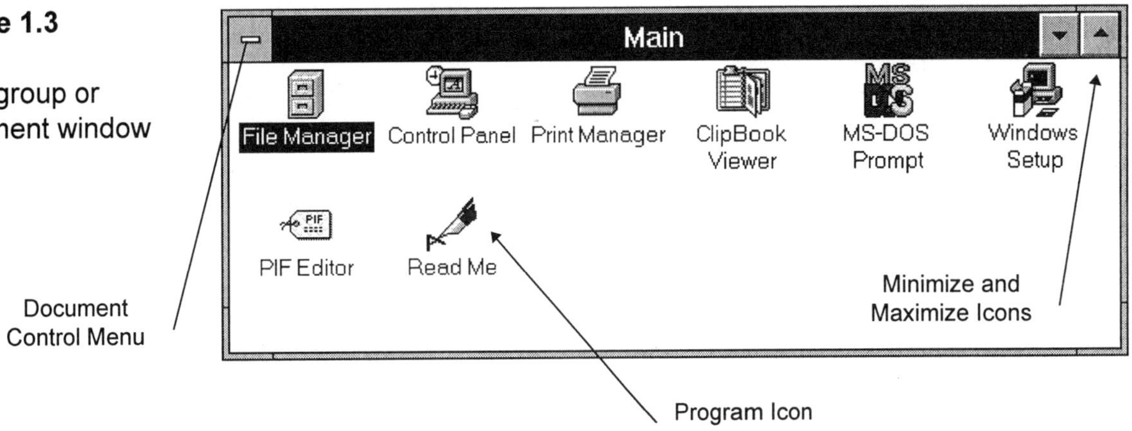

Document Control Menu

Program Icon

EXECUTING PROGRAMS AND COMMANDS

You launch an application program by opening its group window, if necessary, and then double-clicking its icon. Once an application is running, you access its features by choosing commands from the Menu bar and selecting options from dialog boxes.

Menu Bar

Commands are grouped together on a Menu bar, located at the top of most application windows. To execute a command, you first select a menu option and then choose a command from its pull-down menu. Any commands on a pull-down menu that are not available for selection appear dimmed (usually a light gray in color). A check mark beside a command means that the command is currently active or that the feature is turned on.

To access the Menu bar using the mouse, click once on the menu option to display the pull-down menu and then click once on the command you want to execute. To execute a command using the keyboard, press and hold down the [Alt] key and then tap the underlined letter of the desired option on the Menu bar. When the pull-down menu is displayed, press the underlined letter of the command you want to execute.

In this guide commands appear in the following form: File, Open, where File is the Menu bar option and Open is the command you select from the pull-down menu. You can cancel a selection once you are in the Menu bar by pressing the [Esc] key twice. Perform the following steps.

1. To browse the pull-down menus, position the mouse pointer over the File option in the Menu bar.

2. CLICK: left mouse button and hold it down
   The File pull-down menu appears.

3. DRAG: mouse pointer to the right to highlight the other menu options

4. To leave the Menu bar without selecting a command:
   DRAG: mouse pointer to a blank area on the desktop or over the interior of the Program Manager window

5. Release the mouse button.

Dialog Box

A dialog box is a common mechanism in Windows applications for collecting information before processing a command or instruction (Figure 1.4). An ellipsis (...) following a command on a pull-down menu means a dialog box appears when the command is selected. Dialog boxes are also used to display messages or to ask for confirmation of commands.

Figure 1.4

A dialog box

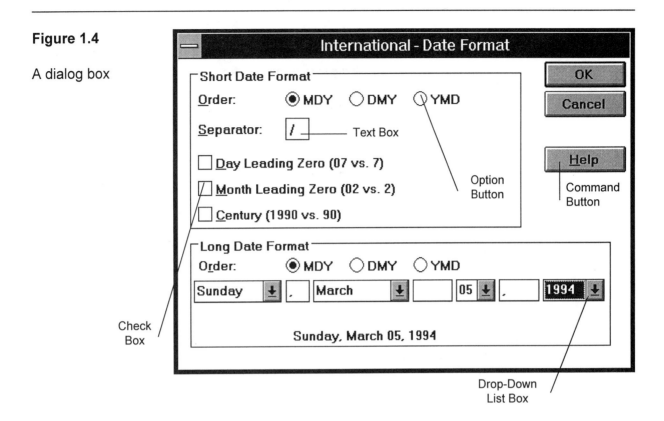

A dialog box uses several methods for collecting information, including list boxes, drop-down list boxes, text boxes, check boxes, option buttons, and command buttons. You can access an item in the dialog box using the mouse or by pressing (Tab) to move clockwise and (Shift)+(Tab) to move counterclockwise around the dialog box.

Study Table 1.2 and Figure 1.4 which show the common elements found in dialog boxes. In the following sessions, you use dialog boxes to choose printers, customize the desktop, manage files, and perform other tasks.

Table 1.2	*Element*	*Description*
Parts of a dialog box	List box	A scrollable list of choices; shows all choices
	Drop-down list box	A scrollable list of choices; shows selected choice only
	Text box	A box for collecting typed information
	Check box	An option that can be turned on or off

Table 1.2
Continued

Element	Description
Option button	One option selected from a group of related options
Command button	A button that executes an action when selected

MANIPULATING WINDOWS

This section introduces methods for sizing, moving, and organizing windows. Similar to shuffling pages on your desk, you position application windows on the Windows desktop so that you can work more efficiently.

SIZING A WINDOW

You size an application or document window by dragging its borders using the mouse. You can also drag the corner of a window frame to size it both horizontally and vertically. In most applications, changing the size of a window does not affect the contents of the window.

You can also maximize or minimize a window by clicking on the icons in the top right-hand corner. The following situations occur when maximizing or minimizing windows:

- Maximizing an application window expands the window to fill the entire screen—no part of the desktop remains visible.
- Maximizing a document window expands the window to fill its application window. The Control menu and Restore icon (▾) for a maximized document window appear beneath the Menu bar.
- When a window is maximized, its Maximize icon (▴) is replaced with a Restore icon (▾) for restoring the window back to its original size.
- Minimizing an application window reduces the window to an icon at the bottom of the desktop.
- Minimizing a document window reduces the window to an icon in its application window.
- When a window is minimized, you restore it to a window by double-clicking on its icon.

To practice sizing windows, perform the following steps.

1. To close the Main group window (assuming that it is already open):
   CLICK: Minimize icon (▼) for the Main group window
   Position the mouse pointer over the icon and click the left mouse button once. Be careful that you do not click the Minimize icon for the Program Manager. (*Note*: If the Main group window is already minimized to an icon in Program Manager, proceed to the next step.)

2. To open the Main group window from an icon:
   DOUBLE-CLICK: Main group icon
   Position the mouse pointer over the icon with "Main" in its title and then press and release the left mouse button twice in rapid succession.

3. To increase the width of the Main group window, first position the mouse pointer over the right vertical border. The mouse pointer changes to a double-headed arrow when positioned correctly.

4. CLICK: left mouse button and hold it down
   DRAG: mouse pointer to the right approximately 1 inch
   You will notice that a shadow of the border frame is moved with the mouse pointer.

5. Release the left mouse button to complete the sizing operation.

6. To decrease the width of the Main group window, position the mouse pointer over the right vertical border until the pointer changes shape.

7. CLICK: left mouse button and hold it down
   DRAG: mouse pointer to the left until the window is 1 inch wide

8. Release the left mouse button. Your screen should appear similar to Figure 1.5.

Figure 1.5

Sizing the Main group window

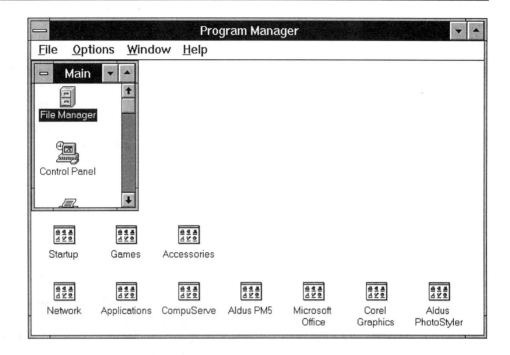

9. To move around the window using the mouse:
   CLICK: arrows at the top and bottom of the vertical scroll bar

10. To move around the window using the Thumb or scroll box, first position the mouse pointer on the scroll box.

11. CLICK: left mouse button and hold it down
    DRAG: mouse pointer and scroll box along the scroll bar

12. Release the mouse button.

Quick Reference *Sizing Windows*	1. Position the mouse pointer on the window's border until the mouse pointer changes to a double-headed arrow. 2. CLICK: the left mouse button and hold it down 3. DRAG: the window frame to increase or decrease its size 4. Release the left mouse button to complete the sizing operation.

MOVING A WINDOW

You move a window by dragging its Title bar using the mouse. Although you can move application windows anywhere on the desktop, document windows are restricted to their application window.

Perform the following steps.

1. Position the mouse pointer on the Main group window's Title bar.

2. To move the window:
   CLICK: left mouse button and hold it down
   DRAG: mouse pointer towards the bottom right-hand corner
   Notice that a shadow of the window frame is moved.

3. When it is positioned correctly, release the left mouse button.

4. Move the window back to its original location.

Quick Reference	1. Position the mouse pointer on the window's Title bar.
Moving Windows	2. CLICK: the left mouse button and hold it down
	3. DRAG: the window frame to a new location
	4. Release the left mouse button to complete the move operation.

ORGANIZING WINDOWS

In addition to moving windows individually, you can automatically arrange all your open windows using the Window menu option. To layer windows like a fanned deck of cards, choose Window, Cascade from the menu. The active window is displayed on top of the other windows in a cascaded arrangement. To display your open windows in a floor tile pattern, choose the Window, Tile command. The active window is placed in the top left-hand corner of the application window and the other windows are tiled next to each other.

Perform the following steps.

1. Open all the group windows by double-clicking on the group icons. (*Note*: If an open window hides a group icon, move the window using the mouse or choose the group from the Window pull-down menu.)

2. To layer the open windows:
   CHOOSE: Window, Cascade
   This instruction tells you to choose the Window option on the Menu bar. Once the pull-down menu appears, you choose the Cascade command. Your screen should now appear similar to Figure 1.6.

Figure 1.6

Cascading open group windows

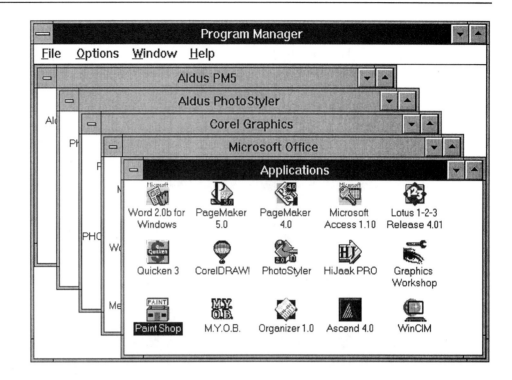

3. CHOOSE: Window, Tile
   Your screen should appear similar to Figure 1.7.

Figure 1.7

Tiling open group windows

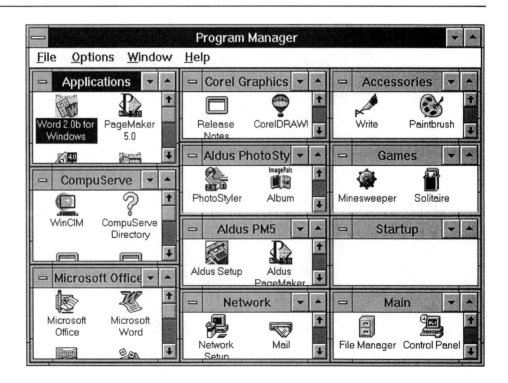

Session 1 21

Quick Reference
Arranging
Windows
	• To arrange windows in a layered format:
	  CHOOSE: Window, Cascade
	• To arrange windows in a tiled format:
	  CHOOSE: Window, Tile

SELECTING WINDOWS

Before issuing a command from an application window's Menu bar, you should first select the document window to be affected by the command. The selected window is called the **active window**. You select a window or make it active by clicking on it using the mouse. Because windows can overlap and become hidden from view, you may have to minimize some windows before you are able to make the desired one active.

Perform the following steps to cycle through the open group windows.

1. CHOOSE: Window, Cascade

2. CLICK: the Title bar of an overlapped window to make it active

3. CHOOSE: Window, Tile

4. CLICK: the Title bar of each window to make it active
   Notice the highlighting of the active Title bar compared to the rest.

PLAYING GAMES

Windows provides two games, Solitaire and Minesweeper, for your enjoyment and to improve your mouse skills.

SOLITAIRE

Solitaire is a computer version of the popular card game. The objective of the game is to place the deck of 52 cards in four suit stacks at the top of the playing board. To do so, you first arrange the cards in descending order, using alternating colors (hearts or diamonds and spades or clubs). You build upon each of the original seven piles using cards from the other piles and the deck. To score points, you place cards in the suit stacks at the top of the screen in ascending order, starting with an Ace. When all cards appear in their respective suit stack, you have won the game. Figure 1.8 shows the Solitaire playing board in the middle of a game.

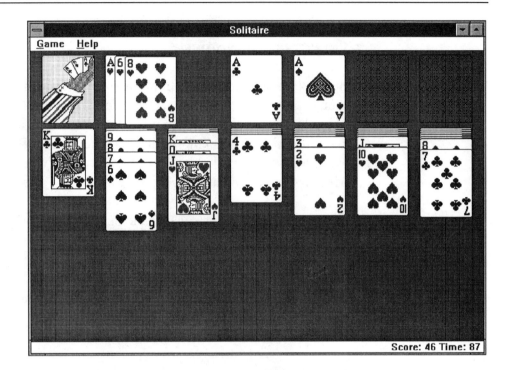

Figure 1.8

The Solitaire playing board

To load Solitaire, open the Games group window and double-click the Solitaire program icon. To flip through the cards, you click the mouse pointer on the top card in the deck. To place a card in the suit stack, you double-click the card on the playing board. To arrange cards from different piles (or from the deck) below a card pile, you drag the card or cards using the mouse. For further assistance, access the Help option in the Menu bar. To quit Solitaire, choose Game, Exit from the menu.

MINESWEEPER

Minesweeper requires strategy and luck to clear the playing board of mines. Using the mouse, you click on squares in the playing field to locate the mines. The total number of mines appears on the left side of the scoreboard and a clock appears on the right side. Through elimination, your mission is to uncover all the squares that do not contain mines.

To start Minesweeper, double-click the Minesweeper program icon in the Games group window. The board appears on the screen with all squares covered. The happy face symbol in the middle of the score board is the Restart button—you click it to restart the game. When you click a square, two events can occur: you survive or you die. If you click a square that does not contain a mine, the square will show a number that is a tally of the mines bordering that square. If you click a square that contains a mine, you lose the game. To quit Minesweeper, choose Game, Exit.

For further information about Minesweeper, access the Help menu option.

EXITING WINDOWS

Always exit Windows before turning off the computer! Windows stores information in a memory area called a *cache*. When you exit Windows properly, it has time to write the contents of the cache to the hard disk for permanent storage. If you shut down your computer before this occurs, you risk losing important information.

If you have arranged the group windows in Program Manager, you can save their new positions using the Options, Save Settings on Exit command. When a check mark appears beside this menu command, the feature is turned on and will save the appearance of your Program Manager whenever you exit Windows. Perform the following steps.

1. To retain the original startup settings and discard the current window positions, ensure that no check mark appears beside the Save Settings on Exit command:
   CHOOSE: Options, Save Settings on Exit

   CAUTION: Ensure that there is not a check mark beside the Save Settings on Exit command before proceeding to the next step.

2. To exit Windows:
   CHOOSE: File, Exit Windows
   PRESS: [Enter] or CLICK: OK
   (*Note*: You can also double-click the Program Manager's Control menu.)

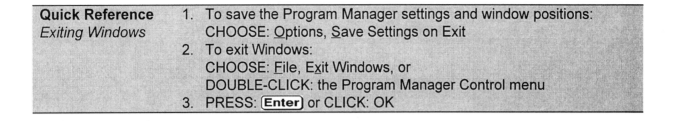

Quick Reference
Exiting Windows

1. To save the Program Manager settings and window positions:
   CHOOSE: Options, Save Settings on Exit
2. To exit Windows:
   CHOOSE: File, Exit Windows, or
   DOUBLE-CLICK: the Program Manager Control menu
3. PRESS: Enter or CLICK: OK

SUMMARY

Microsoft Windows is not an operating system; it's an operating environment that works with DOS to make the computer easier to use. This session introduced you to the advantages of working in Windows and described its primary components: Program Manager, File Manager, Print Manager, Task Manager, and several accessory programs.

In the latter half of the session, you loaded Microsoft Windows and took a guided tour of the main parts of the Windows screen. You sized, moved, and arranged document or group windows. The session concluded with a section on exiting Windows and saving the settings for Program Manager.

Many of the commands and procedures introduced in this session appear in the Command Summary (Table 1.3).

Table 1.3	*Command*	*Description*
Command Summary	Window, Cascade	Layer open windows with the active window on top
	Window, Tile	Arrange open windows in a floor tile format with the active window in the top left-hand corner
	Options, Save Settings on Exit	Save the Program Manager settings and window positions
	File, Exit Windows	Exit Microsoft Windows

KEY TERMS

active window   The document or application window that is currently selected; commands affect the active window only.

application window   In Windows, each running application program appears in its own application window. These windows can be sized and moved anywhere on the Windows desktop.

desktop   The background screen for Windows where you place applications and organize your work.

document window   In Windows, each open document appears in its own document window. These windows can be sized and moved anywhere within the application window.

font   Traditionally, all of the symbols and characters of a typeface for a particular point size. Windows programs use the terms *font* and *typeface* interchangeably to mean all available sizes of a style of print.

graphical user interface   Software feature that allows the user to select menu options and choose icons to perform procedures; makes software easier to use, and generally employs a mouse.

group icons   In Program Manager, icons that represent program groups. To expand the program group into a group window, double-click on the group icon.

group windows   In Program Manager, document windows that contain and organize program item icons.

icons   Pictures or symbols that represent program groups, application programs, files, or other elements on the Windows screen.

mouse   Hand-held input device connected to a microcomputer by a cable; when you slide the mouse across the desk or mouse pad, the mouse pointer or arrow moves across the screen. A button on the mouse allows you to make menu selections and to issue commands.

multitasking   Activity in which more than one task or program is executed at a time. A small amount of each program is processed and then the CPU moves to the remaining programs, one at a time.

program icons In Program Manager, icons that represent application software programs. To execute an application, you double-click the application's program icon.

TrueType Scalable font technology provided with Windows.

typeface A style of print.

WYSIWYG Acronym for *What You See Is What You Get*.

EXERCISES

SHORT ANSWER

1. What is an operating system?
2. What is the difference between a typeface and a font?
3. What is TrueType?
4. What are five advantages of using Windows, as listed in this session?
5. Describe three primary mouse movements in Windows.
6. Describe four common mouse pointer shapes.
7. What is the difference between application and document windows?
8. What happens when you maximize a document or group window?
9. What does it mean to *cascade* the open windows?
10. How can you save the group window positions in Program Manager when you exit Windows?

HANDS-ON

1. This exercise practices manipulating windows in the Program Manager.
    a. Start your computer and load Microsoft Windows.
    b. Close all open group windows in Program Manager.
    c. You will now move each group icon from the bottom of the application window to the top—directly underneath the Menu bar. To begin, position the mouse pointer over a group icon.
    d. DRAG: group icon to the top of the application window
    e. Release the mouse button.
    f. Repeat the drag operation for each icon until they are all lined up near the top of the application window.

Session 1   27

   g. Open the Main group window.
   h. Size the Main group window to approximately 2- by 2-inches.
   i. Position the mouse pointer on the Title bar of the Main group window.
   j. Move the window to the top right-hand corner of the Program Manager window by dragging the window frame.
   k. Move the window into the center of the Program Manager window. Your screen should now appear similar to Figure 1.9.

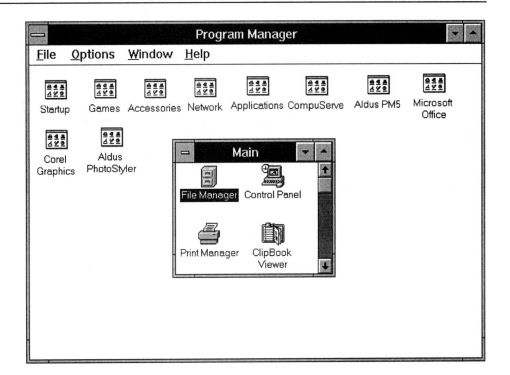

Figure 1.9

Moving and sizing the Main group window

2. In this exercise, you maximize, minimize, cascade, and tile group windows in the Program Manager.
   a. Ensure that the Main group window is the only open window in the Program Manager application window.
   b. Open the other group windows using the mouse:
      DOUBLE-CLICK: *all group icons*
   c. Cascade the open windows.
   d. Tile the open windows.
   e. Close all the open group windows by double-clicking their Control menus. (*Note*: Make sure you do not double-click the Program Manager's Control menu.)
   f. Open the Main group window only.

g. Maximize the Main group window:
   CLICK: Maximize icon in the Main group window
   Notice how the Main group window's Title bar melds with the Program Manager Title bar. Also note that there is a Restore icon in the top right-hand corner of the Program Manager window, immediately below the application window's Maximize icon.
h. Restore the Main group to a window:
   CLICK: Restore icon
i   Open up Accessories group window.
j. Open up StartUp group window.
k. Using the mouse, organize the open group windows to match the display in Figure 1.10.

Figure 1.10

Arranging open group windows

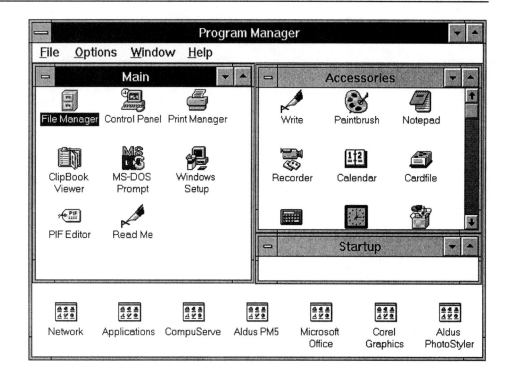

l. Close all the open group windows.
m. Exit Windows.

SESSION 2

SIMPLY WINDOWS: WORKING WITH WINDOWS

Microsoft Windows lets you concentrate on getting things done rather than worrying about how to do things. Similar to the way you work at your own desk, you can open project folders in Windows, set them aside temporarily to write a letter or calculate a bill, and then return later to pick up where you left off. Adding new printers, customizing your work area, getting help, and managing application programs is easy with Program Manager, as shown in this session.

PREVIEW

When you have completed this session, you will be able to:

Name the program icons contained in the Main and Accessories group windows.

•

Create a new group window and copy program items.

•

Change the color of the Windows screen.

•

Display a pattern or graphic on the desktop.

•

Select and customize the default printer.

•

Use Print Manager to manipulate files in the print queue.

•

Retrieve context-sensitive help.

SESSION OUTLINE

Why This Session Is Important
Program Manager
    The StartUp Group
    Creating a New Group
    Deleting Groups and Program Items
Control Panel
    Choosing a Color Scheme
    Customizing the Desktop
    Using a Screen Saver
    Choosing a Printer
Print Manager
Getting Help
Summary
    Command Summary
Key Terms
Exercises
    Short Answer
    Hands-On

Session 2 31

WHY THIS SESSION IS IMPORTANT

This session introduces Program Manager, Control Panel, Print Manager, and the Windows Help facility. Program Manager helps you manage your application programs. In this session, you learn how to create your own group window in the Program Manager window. With Control Panel and Print Manager, you learn how to customize your desktop and set up your printers. Lastly, this session introduces you to the Windows Help facility for retrieving on-line help information.

Before proceeding, make sure the following are true:

1. You have turned on your computer system and loaded Windows.
2. The Program Manager window appears on the screen.
3. Your Advantage Diskette is inserted into drive A:. You will work with files on the diskette that have been created for you. (*Note*: The Advantage Diskette can be duplicated by copying all of the files from your instructor's Master Advantage Diskette.)

PROGRAM MANAGER

Windows enables you to organize your application programs into groups. Each application program and group is represented by an icon in Program Manager. When first installed, Windows automatically sets up several groups for you, including Main and Accessories. The program items in these groups are listed alphabetically in Table 2.1.

Table 2.1
Windows Program Items

Name	Icon	Description
Calculator	🔢	General or scientific calculator
Calendar	📅	Daily diary and monthly planner program
Cardfile	🗂	Small database program for storing phone numbers, addresses, or other information

Table 2.1 (continued)

Name	Icon	Description
Character Map		Series of special symbols that you can insert into documents and applications
Clipboard		Clipboard viewer for displaying data that appears in the memory buffer
Clock		Analog or digital clock
Control Panel		System program for setting screen and printer defaults and other configuration options
File Manager		File and disk management program for copying files and formatting disks
Media Player		Utility for playing MIDI audio files; a multimedia extension
Minesweeper		Game
MS-DOS Prompt		DOS command prompt
Notepad		Small text editor for creating system initialization files (INI) and batch files (BAT)
Object Packager		Program that creates objects for sharing and exchanging information between applications
Paintbrush		Drawing program for creating, saving, and printing graphic pictures
PIF Editor		Program for creating Program Information Files for DOS applications
Print Manager		Program that manages jobs or documents sent to the printer
Recorder		Macro recorder for saving keystrokes and mouse actions for later playback
Solitaire		Klondike Solitaire game

Table 2.1 (continued)	Name	Icon	Description
	Sound Recorder		Program that records and plays back sounds; plays and edits audio WAV files
	Terminal		Communications program for connecting to other computers using a modem
	Write		Word processing program for creating, saving, and printing documents, such as letters

THE STARTUP GROUP

The StartUp group lets you specify programs that you want automatically launched each time you start Windows. Unlike the Main and Accessories groups, the StartUp group window is initially empty when you first install Windows onto your hard disk. To place or copy a program icon into the StartUp group, you press and hold down the Ctrl key as you drag the icon from its original window to the StartUp group window. You will get an opportunity to practice this technique in the next section.

CREATING A NEW GROUP

Program Manager lets you create your own group windows and program items in addition to the standard groups and programs provided by Windows. This feature lets you group together your most frequently accessed programs into a single group window.

Perform the following steps to create your own application group.

1. Close all the open group windows in Program Manager.

2. To create a new application group called *My Apps*:
   CHOOSE: File, New

The following dialog box appears:

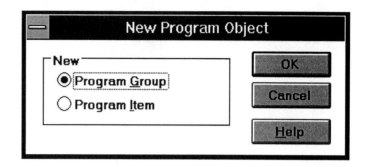

3. SELECT: Program Group option button

4. PRESS: [Enter] or CLICK: OK
   The Program Group Properties dialog box appears for you to enter the name of the new application group.

5. In the Description text box, enter the name that will appear beneath the application group's icon and in its Title bar:
   TYPE: My Apps
   PRESS: [Enter] or CLICK: OK
   A new group window appears with the Title bar "My Apps."

6. Open the Main group window.

7. CHOOSE: Window, Tile

8. To copy the File Manager icon from the Main group window to the My Apps group window:
   PRESS: [Ctrl] and hold it down
   DRAG: File Manager icon (🗃) from Main to My Apps

9. When the mouse pointer and icon appear over the My Apps window, release the mouse button and [Ctrl] key to complete the copy.

10. Using the same process as described in steps 8 and 9, copy Clock and Calculator from the Accessories group window into the My Apps window. Your screen should appear similar to Figure 2.1.

Session 2   35

Figure 2.1

The My Apps group window

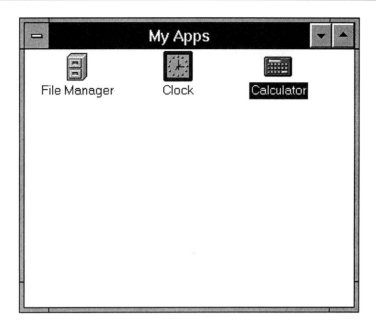

Quick Reference	1. CHOOSE: File, New
Creating a New	2. SELECT: Program Group or Program Item option button
Application Group	3. PRESS: [Enter] or CLICK: OK
or Program Item	4. TYPE: *the desired icon title in the Description text box*
	5. PRESS: [Enter] or CLICK: OK

DELETING GROUPS AND PROGRAM ITEMS

You remove a program item or application group window by selecting the desired icon and pressing [Delete]. When asked for confirmation of the deletion, you respond by selecting Yes in the dialog box to permanently remove the program or group. You can also use the File, Delete command.

Perform the following steps.

1. CLICK: Calculator icon in the My Apps window once

2. To remove this program item:
   PRESS: [Delete]

The following dialog box appears:

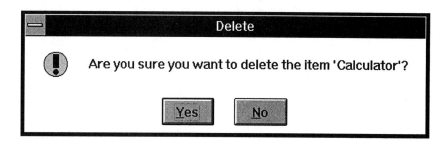

3. Ensure that you are deleting the copied Calculator icon that appears in the My Apps group window. If correct, confirm the deletion:
CLICK: Yes

4. Remove the Clock icon and File Manager icon from the My Apps group window.

5. To remove the My Apps group window:
PRESS: [Delete]
CLICK: Yes command button to confirm the deletion
Because there were no program items left to delete, Windows correctly assumed that you wanted to delete the group window itself.

Quick Reference *Removing a Program Item or Application Group*	1. SELECT: the program item icon, group window, or group icon 2. PRESS: [Delete], or CHOOSE: File, Delete 3. PRESS: [Enter] or CLICK: Yes to confirm the deletion

CONTROL PANEL

With Control Panel, you can change the system defaults for your computer and printers. You can also customize the appearance of the desktop using color schemes, background patterns, bitmap graphics, and screen savers. To launch Control Panel, open the Main group window and then double-click on the Control Panel program icon. The Control Panel dialog box is similar to a special group window that contains several configuration programs. Most of these program item icons are listed in Table 2.2.

Table 2.2

Control Panel Icons

Name	Icon	Configuration Task
Color		Select predefined color schemes or create your own color combinations for the screen
Date/Time		Change the system date and time for the computer's internal clock
Desktop		Specify a pattern or wallpaper graphic for the desktop and implement a screen saver utility
Drivers		Set up multimedia hardware components and software drivers
Fonts		Define screen and printer fonts; add new fonts
International		Change the keyboard layout, date and time display, and currency format
Keyboard		Specify the keyboard speed and repeat rate
Mouse		Set mouse tracking and double-clicking speeds or swap the left and right mouse buttons
Ports		Specify communication parameters for serial ports COM1, COM2, COM3, and COM4
Printers		Select and configure the default printer and specify whether to use Print Manager
Sound		Assign sounds (WAV files) to Windows events
386 Enhanced		If you are using a 386 or better computer in enhanced mode, this program lets you set the processing and virtual memory options

CHOOSING A COLOR SCHEME

Whether you use a 17-inch color monitor, 12-inch monochrome monitor, or liquid crystal display (LCD screens are common in laptop and notebook computers), you will appreciate the variety of color schemes available for

Windows. While seemingly superficial, the ability to change colors is especially significant for notebook users who generally have VGA color capabilities with gray-scale LCD screens. To avoid eyestrain and improve the aesthetic appeal of Windows, you can pick and choose the best color combinations for enhancing your screen's overall brightness and clarity.

Perform the following steps to change the Windows color scheme.

1. Open the Main group window.

2. Open the Control Panel dialog box:
   DOUBLE-CLICK: Control Panel icon (🖳)

3. To change the color scheme, select the Color option:
   DOUBLE-CLICK: Color icon (III)
   The Color dialog box appears.

4. To select a predefined color scheme:
   SELECT: Color Schemes drop-down list box
   (*Note*: You select the drop-down list box by clicking the down arrow that appears to the right of the box.)

5. To sample the various color schemes:
   PRESS: ↓ multiple times to scroll through the list
   Notice that the sample window below the drop-down list box displays the highlighted color selection.

6. SELECT: *your favorite color scheme*

7. Save your selection and return to the Control Panel dialog box:
   PRESS: Enter or CLICK: OK

You can also select custom colors for individual screen elements, such as borders, Title bars, and windows. To select custom colors, you choose the Color Palette command button in the Color dialog box. The dialog box expands to display a palette of colors (Figure 2.2). To apply a custom color to a screen element, you click the screen element in the sample window and then click the desired color from the palette. When finished selecting colors, you save your custom color scheme with the other Windows schemes by choosing the Save Scheme command button.

Figure 2.2

Selecting custom colors from the Color dialog box

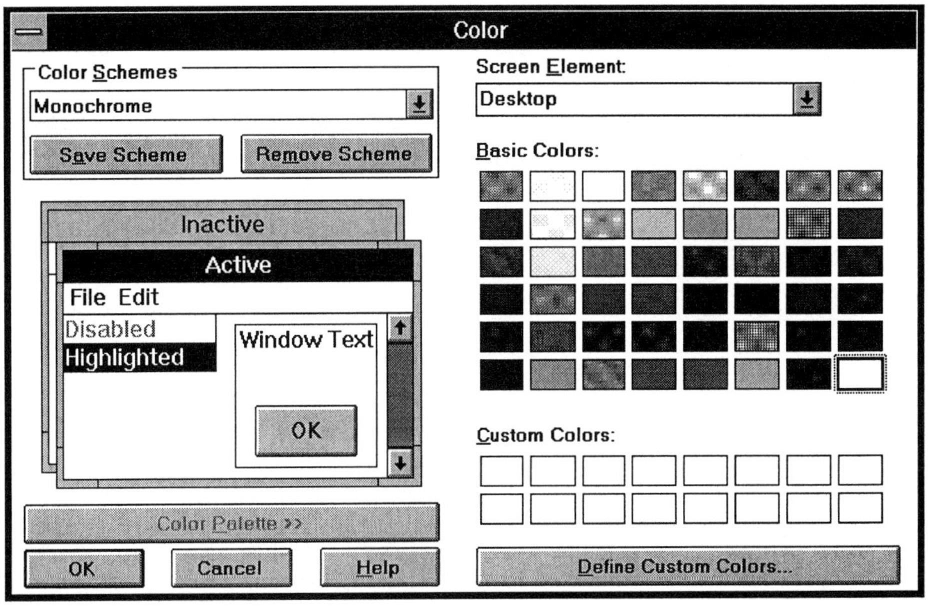

Quick Reference	1. DOUBLE-CLICK: Color icon from the Control Panel dialog box
Choosing a Color Scheme	2. SELECT: a predefined color scheme from the drop-down list box
	3. PRESS: [Enter] or CLICK: OK

CUSTOMIZING THE DESKTOP

You can customize the appearance of the Windows desktop using patterns or **bitmap graphics** (images stored in disk files.) To display a pattern or bitmap graphic on the desktop, select the Desktop icon from the Control Panel dialog box. In the Desktop dialog box (Figure 2.3), select the name of the desired pattern or specify a file containing the bitmap graphic for wallpapering the desktop. You are not limited to using the bitmap graphics provided by Windows for your wallpaper. In fact, many organizations use a bitmap graphic of their company logo for wallpaper.

Figure 2.3

The Desktop dialog box

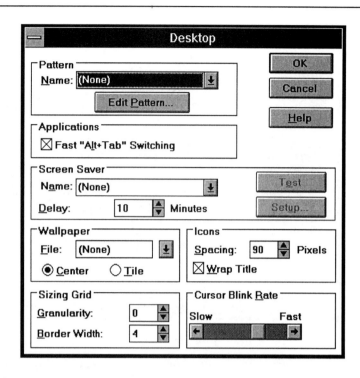

Perform the following steps.

1. Ensure that the Control Panel dialog box is displayed.

2. To apply a pattern to the desktop:
   DOUBLE-CLICK: Desktop icon

3. To select a pattern:
   SELECT: Name drop-down list box in the Pattern area

4. To browse through the available patterns:
   CLICK: up and down arrows on the scroll bar of the drop-down list

5. CHOOSE: Critters pattern option

6. In the Wallpaper drop-down list box:
   SELECT: (None)

7. To view the pattern:
   PRESS: [Enter] or CLICK: OK

8. To better see the desktop, minimize Program Manager. Do not, however, minimize the Control Panel dialog box.

Session 2

9. To select a bitmap graphic for wallpapering the desktop:
   DOUBLE-CLICK: Desktop icon in the Control Panel dialog box

10. To display the wallpaper bitmap graphic options:
    SELECT: (None) in the Pattern area to remove the previous selection
    SELECT: File drop-down list box in the Wallpaper area
    CLICK: up and down arrows on the scroll bar of the drop-down list

11. CHOOSE: WINLOGO.BMP from the list of wallpaper options

12. SELECT: Tile option button
    The Tile option reproduces the bitmap graphic until it fills the entire desktop screen. The Center option places only one copy of the bitmap graphic in the center of the screen.

13. PRESS: [Enter] or CLICK: OK
    You should see the Windows logo etched into the desktop.

14. DOUBLE-CLICK: Desktop icon in the Control Panel dialog box

15. Practice selecting other options from the Wallpaper area.

16. Before proceeding, do the following:
    DOUBLE-CLICK: Desktop icon in the Control Panel dialog box
    SELECT: (None) in the Wallpaper area
    PRESS: [Enter] or CLICK: OK

17. Close the Control Panel dialog box.

18. To restore the Program Manager window:
    DOUBLE-CLICK: Program Manager icon

Quick Reference	1. DOUBLE-CLICK: Desktop icon from the Control Panel dialog box
Choosing a Desktop Pattern or Wallpaper	2. SELECT: *the name of a background pattern or specify a file containing a bitmap graphic for wallpapering the desktop*
	3. PRESS: [Enter] or CLICK: OK

USING A SCREEN SAVER

Windows provides a screen saver utility that helps to protect the life of your monitor and the security of your system. When a static, unchanging screen image is displayed on the monitor for extended periods of time, the image may become etched into the monitor. A screen saver program automatically blanks your screen, or displays random moving objects, to avoid burning in a screen image on the monitor when it is left on for prolonged periods of time. The Windows screen saver also incorporates password protection, which requires you to enter a password before removing the screen saver utility and returning you to your work.

Perform the following steps.

1. Open the Control Panel dialog box.

2. To select a screen saver for Windows:
   DOUBLE-CLICK: Desktop icon

3. SELECT: Name drop-down list box in the Screen Saver area

4. To browse through the available screen savers:
   CLICK: up and down arrows on the scroll bar of the drop-down list

5. CHOOSE: Mystify option

6. To test the screen saver:
   CLICK: Test command button
   The screen blanks and displays the selected screen saver option. You may need to click the mouse button again to return to the dialog box.

7. In the Delay box, you enter the number of minutes that should elapse without activity before displaying the screen saver. For this example, set the value to 10 minutes.

8. PRESS: [Enter] or CLICK: OK

Quick Reference
Choosing a Screen Saver

1. DOUBLE-CLICK: Desktop icon from the Control Panel dialog box
2. SELECT: *a screen saver from the Name drop-down list box in the Screen Saver area*
3. CLICK: Test command button to view the screen saver
4. Specify the amount of time to wait before initiating the screen saver by entering a number in the Delay text box.
5. PRESS: [Enter] or CLICK: OK

CHOOSING A PRINTER

The Printers option in the Control Panel dialog box enables you to add, modify, and remove **printer drivers**, the files that enable a program to communicate with various types of printers. To specify a default printer, you select the desired printer and choose the Set as Default Printer command button in the Printers dialog box (Figure 2.4). In the bottom left-hand corner, make sure the check box is selected to use the Print Manager. If Print Manager is not selected, you must wait for one document to finish printing before sending another document to the printer.

To customize the settings for the default printer, select the Setup button to specify the paper source, number of copies to print, and **orientation** (in portrait orientation the page is printed upright similar to this page; in landscape it prints sideways).

Figure 2.4

Printers dialog box

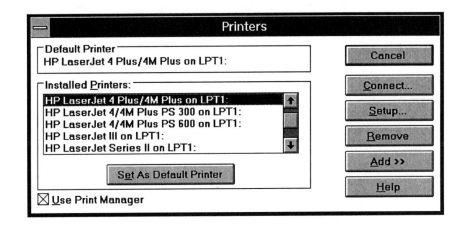

PRINT MANAGER

In a multitasking environment, application programs must share processing time, memory, and printer resources. Windows manages your system resources using programs like Print Manager. To coordinate the printing of multiple documents, Print Manager places documents temporarily in a print spooler or **queue** on the hard disk. When the printer has completed one print job, Print Manager takes the next print job from the queue and feeds it to the printer. Because this spooling process occurs in the background, you can continue working in an application immediately after you send a document to the printer.

With Print Manager, you can monitor the active and inactive printers and the status of files that have been sent to the print queue. Figure 2.5 shows the Print Manager window with three files sent to the HP printer attached to LPT1, while the other printers remain idle. (*Note*: The following screen graphic of the Print Manager window is taken from Windows for Workgroups 3.11. Your screen may differ.)

Figure 2.5

Print Manager window

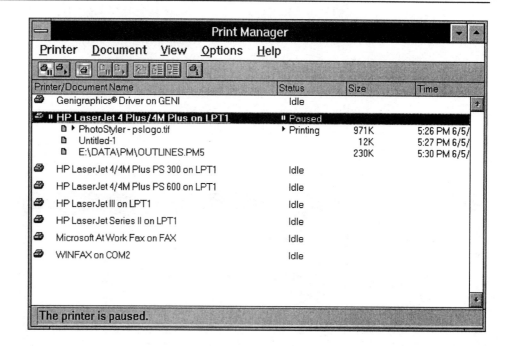

You can manipulate the print queue in Print Manager by reordering and deleting files that appear in the list. For example, if you want to print a one-page letter after sending several larger documents to the printer, you can move the letter up in the print queue so that it is the next document in line for the printer. To move a file in the queue, you simply drag the file name using the mouse. You delete a file from the queue by selecting the file and then clicking on the Delete button or icon under the Menu bar.

GETTING HELP

Because you may not always remember the steps needed to perform an operation, Windows provides an extensive on-line Help facility. To retrieve context-sensitive help at any time, you simply press the F1 key.

Context-sensitive refers to Windows' ability to retrieve Help information for your current position in the program. The Help option on the Program Manager Menu bar allows you to access specific Help topics (Table 2.3).

Table 2.3 Help Menu	Command	Description
	<u>C</u>ontents	A topical index for getting help for Program Manager
	<u>S</u>earch for Help on	A search facility for looking up Help information
	<u>H</u>ow to Use Help	Information on using the Help facility
	<u>W</u>indows Tutorial	Tutorial for using the mouse and manipulating windows
	<u>A</u>bout Program Manager	Displays version, mode, and memory information

Once a Help window is displayed, Windows provides several command buttons to control movement through the Help facility: Contents, Search, Back, History, and Glossary. Selecting the Contents button or Search button performs the same procedure as choosing their respective menu options. The Back button enables you to see the previous Help topic and the History button provides a scrollable list of all the topics you have viewed in the session. If you need to look up a word's definition, the Glossary button displays a glossary of terms in alphabetical order.

When you access a Help window (Figure 2.6), you may notice some words or phrases that have a solid or dotted underline. A solid underline denotes a **jump term** that you can select to jump to another Help topic for additional information. A word or phrase that has a dotted underline provides a definition box when selected.

Figure 2.6

Help facility

Perform the following steps to access the Help facility.

1. To display a directory of the Help facility contents:
   CHOOSE: Help, Contents

2. To retrieve help on quitting Windows:
   CLICK: Quit Windows topic under the How To... section

3. After reading the Help information, close the window:
   CHOOSE: File, Exit
   (*Note*: You can also double-click the Control menu for the Program Manager Help window.)

4. To display memory status and copyright information:
   CHOOSE: Help, About Program Manager

5. After reading the information:
   PRESS: (Enter) or CLICK: OK

Quick Reference	• PRESS: (F1) to display context-sensitive help
Using Help	• CHOOSE: Help, Contents to display a list of Help topics
	• CHOOSE: Help, About to display memory and copyright information

SUMMARY

Building on the skills you learned in Session 1, this session explored more features of the Program Manager. You not only created a new program group but added several program items to the window. This session also introduced the Control Panel for setting up and customizing Windows. You examined the Color option for changing the screen colors, the Desktop option for choosing desktop patterns and wallpaper, and the Printers option for specifying and configuring printers. Brief sections on Print Manager and the Windows Help facility concluded the session.

Many of the commands and procedures introduced in this session appear in the Command Summary (Table 2.4).

Table 2.4

Command Summary

Command	Description
File, New	Create a new program group or program item
File, Delete	Delete a program group or program item
Help, *command*	Retrieve information from the Windows Help facility

KEY TERMS

bitmap graphics   A graphic image or picture that is stored in a disk file as a series or pattern of dots.

context-sensitive   Refers to Windows' ability to provide help for your current position in the program.

jump term   In the Windows Help facility, click on a jump term to move to another Help topic. Jump terms are underlined with a solid line.

orientation   Describes how a page is printed. Letter-size paper with a portrait orientation measures 8.5" wide by 11" high. Letter-size paper with a landscape orientation measures 11" wide by 8.5" high.

printer drivers Files stored on a disk containing instructions that enable a software program to communicate with a printer.

queue An area of Print Manager that uses memory and the disk to line up and prioritize documents waiting for the printer.

EXERCISES

SHORT ANSWER

1. What is the purpose of the StartUp program group?
2. How do you copy a program icon from one group window to another?
3. Which two options appear when you choose File, New from the Program Manager menu?
4. How do you change the color scheme of your Windows desktop?
5. What is meant by the phrase *wallpaper your desktop*?
6. What are two benefits of using the Windows screen saver?
7. What must you do to ensure that the Print Manager program handles the printing of your documents?
8. How do you change the order of documents once they appear in the Print Manager queue?
9. In a Help window, explain the difference between a term that has a solid underline and one that has a dotted underline.
10. Explain how *jump terms* work in the Windows Help facility.

HANDS-ON

(*Note*: In the following exercises, you perform Windows commands using files located on the Advantage Diskette.)

1. This exercise practices creating program groups.
   a. Start your computer and load Microsoft Windows.
   b. Ensure that the Advantage Diskette is placed into drive A:.
   c. Close all open group windows.
   d. Create a new group window for your business documents called Business Folder.
   e. To reposition the window:
      CHOOSE: Window, Cascade

Session 2

f. To add a program item to the new group window:
CHOOSE: File, New
SELECT: Program Item option
PRESS: (Enter) or CLICK: OK

g. In the Program Item Properties dialog box, you enter the program file name and any other parameters for the new program item. For this exercise, you will create a program item that uses the Windows Notepad program to read a text file on the Advantage Diskette. To begin, enter the name for the program item in the Description box:
TYPE: Example Business Document
PRESS: (Tab)

h. In the Command Line dialog box, you enter the program filename and the document filename, separated by a space:
TYPE: notepad.exe a:\example.txt
PRESS: (Enter) or CLICK: OK

A program icon, modeled after the Notepad application icon, appears in the group window. (*Note*: Don't worry if you are confused by this step. This exercise merely demonstrates what you can do with program items. You are not expected to know the names of the Windows programs, such as NOTEPAD.EXE.) Your screen should appear similar to Figure 2.7 before continuing.

Figure 2.7

Creating a program item icon in the Business Folder's group window

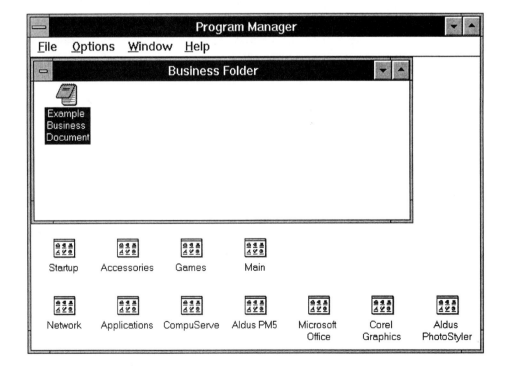

i. To see how this program item works:
   DOUBLE-CLICK: Example Business Document icon
   After a few moments, the Notepad program opens the EXAMPLE.TXT file that appears on the Advantage Diskette.
j. CHOOSE: File, Exit from the Notepad window
k. To clean house in the Program Manager window, delete the Example Business Document program icon and the Business Folder group window:
   PRESS: [Delete]
   CLICK: Yes to confirm the deletion of the program item
   PRESS: [Delete]
   CLICK: Yes to confirm the deletion of the group window

2. This exercise practices customizing the desktop using the pattern and wallpaper options.
   a. Open the Control Panel dialog box from the Main group window.
   b. DOUBLE-CLICK: Desktop icon
   c. To specify a background pattern for the desktop:
      SELECT: Quilt option from the Name drop-down list box
      PRESS: [Enter] or CLICK: OK
      You should see the pattern change on the background screen. If the pattern does not appear on the desktop, make sure that the Wallpaper option in the Desktop dialog box is set to (None).
   d. Minimize the Program Manager window.
   e. To display a bitmap graphic on the desktop:
      DOUBLE-CLICK: Desktop option
   f. For patterns, specify (None) in the Name drop-down list box.
   g. To specify a bitmap graphic for the desktop:
      SELECT: CASTLE.BMP option from the File drop-down list box
      PRESS: [Enter] or CLICK: OK
   h. Return to the Desktop dialog box and select (None) in the Wallpaper area before proceeding.

3. In this exercise, you navigate the Help facility to retrieve information on several topics.
   a. Browse the contents of the Microsoft Windows Help facility. Start by choosing the Help, Contents command from the Program Manager application window.
   b. Under the How To section in the Help window:
      CLICK: Organize Applications and Documents option
   c. CLICK: Changing Properties option

Session 2

    d. Notice that there are two words in the first sentence that have dotted underlines. To view the definition for *program item*, position the hand-shaped mouse pointer over the words and click the left mouse button once.
    e. After reading the definition, remove the definition box:
       CLICK: definition box
    f. View the definition for *group*.
    g. After reading the definition, remove the definition box.
    h. To return to the contents area:
       CLICK: Contents button under the Menu bar
    i. Under the How To section:
       CLICK: Change an Icon
    j. To view a list of all the Help topics that you have selected:
       CLICK: History button
       Your screen should now appear similar to Figure 2.8.

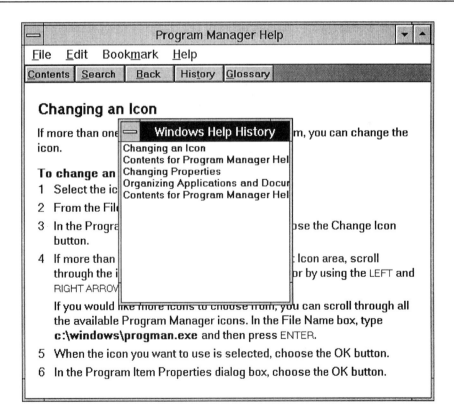

Figure 2.8

History dialog box displayed with a Help Window

    k. Close the Windows Help History dialog box.
    l. Return to the contents area.
    m. To display the Windows Help Glossary:
       CLICK: Glossary button

n. Look up the word *wallpaper* and write down the exact definition as it appears in the glossary.
o. Close the Glossary dialog box.
p. Close the Help facility.

SESSION 3

SIMPLY WINDOWS: USING WRITE AND OTHER ACCESSORY PROGRAMS

You typically use several tools to accomplish your daily work tasks. A landscaper uses a pick, shovel, and hoe to create a garden, while an accountant uses a columnar pad, pencil, and calculator to analyze a budget. The tools that you have available often determine your productivity in a job. How productive would the landscaper or accountant be without their shovel or calculator? Microsoft understands this correlation between tools and productivity, which is why they included several accessory programs in the Windows package.

PREVIEW

When you have completed this session, you will be able to:

Use the Write word processing program to create, edit, format, print, and save documents.

•

Use Paintbrush to draw and manipulate graphic images.

•

Describe the accessory programs that are bundled with Microsoft Windows.

•

Multitask and manage several applications programs.

•

Use the Clipboard to copy information.

SESSION OUTLINE

Why This Session Is Important
Using Write
    Creating a Document
    Saving a Document
    Opening an Existing Document
    Selecting and Editing Text
    Formatting Text
    Printing a Document
    Leaving Write
Using Paintbrush
Using Other Accessories
Multitasking
Summary
    Command Summary
Key Terms
Exercises
    Short Answer
    Hands-On

Why This Session Is Important

Microsoft Windows provides the working environment or shell for application programs such as Word, Excel, and PageMaker. Windows also provides several accessory programs which can be categorized as full applications, personal productivity tools, system utilities, and multimedia tools. For full applications, Windows provides the Write word processing program, the Paintbrush paint program, and the Terminal communications program. Personal productivity tools include the Windows Clock, Calculator, Cardfile, and Calendar programs. System utilities are programs that you use to accomplish tasks in other programs and include the Character Map program, Object Packager, Notepad, and Recorder. In the multimedia category, Windows provides Media Player and Sound Recorder. *Multimedia* is used primarily for corporate and educational presentations and is defined as the combination of different types of media, such as text, sound, animation, and video.

In this session, you are introduced to several accessory programs. Although some sections provide only a brief introduction to a program, you can access the Help menu option for further on-line assistance.

Before proceeding, make sure the following are true:

1. You have turned on your computer system and loaded Windows 3.1.
2. The Program Manager window appears on the screen.
3. Your Advantage Diskette is inserted into drive A:. You will work with files on the diskette that have been created for you. (*Note*: The Advantage Diskette can be duplicated by copying all of the files from your instructor's Master Advantage Diskette.)

Using Write

Word processing is the most commonly used application for microcomputers. Using the Windows Write word processing program, you can store, retrieve, edit, format, and print various types of documents. One significant advantage that word processing software programs have compared to typewriters is a feature called **word wrap**. Word wrap is the automatic process of moving the cursor to the next line when the end of the current line is reached. In other words, you type continuously without pressing the carriage return or **Enter** key to advance to the next line. In Write, the **Enter** key is used to end paragraphs and insert blank lines.

To load Windows Write, you choose the Write program icon in the Accessories group window. Once the program loads, you are presented with the Write window (Figure 3.1), ready for typing information or retrieving a document file.

Figure 3.1

Windows Write word processing program

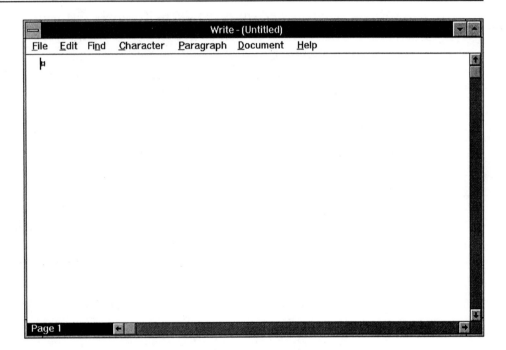

CREATING A DOCUMENT

Creating a document using Windows Write is easy. You type information onto the screen, save the document to the disk, and then send it to the printer. Before entering text into the document, make sure that you have a blinking cursor (also called an **insertion point**) in the upper left-hand corner of the Write window. This marks the location where text is inserted. To the right of the cursor, you should see a small symbol called the **End mark**. Although the cursor cannot be moved below this mark, the mark automatically moves downward as you enter text.

Session 3

To create a simple document, perform the following steps:

1. Open the Accessories group window and then double-click the Write program icon (✍). A blank document appears so that you can begin typing.

2. TYPE: `Word Processing`

3. To insert a blank line between the heading and the body text:
   PRESS: [Enter] twice

4. TYPE: `For some people the concept of writing using a computer is difficult to grasp. These people are accustomed to using the traditional tools for word processing -- paper and pen, pencil, or typewriter. It's natural to think that a new way of doing things is going to be difficult. However, once you have worked through this session, you'll wonder how you ever managed without a computer.`

   (*Note*: If you make a mistake when you are typing the paragraph, press the [BackSpace] key to erase the mistake and retype the correct text. To correct previous mistakes, position the insertion point to the left of the word that you want to remove and press [Delete] several times until the word disappears. When you type in the new word, the existing text is pushed to the right.)

5. PRESS: [Enter]

SAVING A DOCUMENT

When you create or edit a document, you are working in the computer's temporary memory. To permanently store your work in a file on a disk, you choose File, Save or File, Save As from the menu. You are then prompted by Write to name your file using up to eight characters with no spaces. Examples of valid file names are FAX01 and PROPOSAL.

Perform the following steps to save the practice paragraph.

1. Ensure that the Advantage Diskette is placed into drive A:.

2. CHOOSE: File, Save As
   The File, Save and File, Save As commands are identical if the document has never been saved before. If a document has been previously saved, you use the Save command to save modifications to a document over the existing version. The Save As command is used to specify a new file name or to designate a different disk drive.

3. Enter the file name:
   TYPE: a:practice
   PRESS: Enter or CLICK: OK
   Notice that the drive letter is placed before the file name to ensure that the file is saved onto the Advantage Diskette in drive A:.

When working on an important document, you should save the document every 15 minutes to protect yourself against a surprise power outage or other catastrophe.

Quick Reference	1. CHOOSE: File, Save or File, Save As
Saving a Document	2. If the file has never been saved before, enter a file name.
	3. PRESS: Enter or CLICK: OK

OPENING AN EXISTING DOCUMENT

To modify or print a document that is stored on a disk, you must first retrieve the file using the File, Open command. Once the Open dialog box is displayed, you select the appropriate drive and directory and then double-click the document name appearing in the list box (Figure 3.2). You can also type the document name in the File Name text box and then press Enter or click on OK.

Figure 3.2

The File Open dialog box

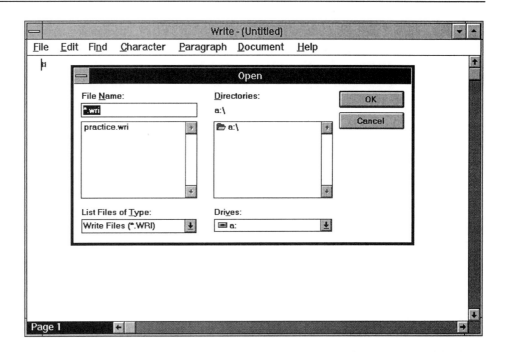

Quick Reference	1. CHOOSE: File, Open
Opening an	2. SELECT: *the appropriate drive and directory*
Existing Document	3. DOUBLE-CLICK: *the desired file name*

SELECTING AND EDITING TEXT

Once text has been typed into a document, editing and formatting changes are made by first selecting the text and then issuing the appropriate command. Selected text always appears highlighted in reverse video. In other words, selected text appears white on black if your video display is normally black on white. A selection may be comprised of letters, words, lines, paragraphs, or the entire document.

MOVING AROUND A DOCUMENT There are better ways to move around a document than pressing the [↑] and [↓] cursor-movement keys. Although these keys work well in short documents, they are not efficient for multiple page documents. For these cases, you should use the mouse and scroll bar. To page down or up through a document, you click the mouse pointer on the scroll bar below or above the scroll box, respectively. You can also drag the scroll box along the scroll bar to move more than one page at a time. Clicking the arrow heads at the top and bottom of the scroll bar enable you to move the contents of the window one line at a time.

SELECTING TEXT   Write provides a column in the left margin of the document window called the **Selection area**. Although invisible, this area provides shortcuts for selecting text using the mouse. When the mouse is moved into this area, the pointer changes from an I-beam to a right-pointing diagonal arrow. Some methods for selecting a word, line, paragraph, or the entire document using the mouse are summarized in Table 3.1. To extend the selection to include several words, lines, or paragraphs, make the initial selection and then hold down the left mouse button and drag the pointer over the desired text.

Table 3.1	*Select*	*Description*
Selecting Text Using the Mouse	Single letter	Position the I-beam pointer to the left of the letter you want to select. Press down and hold the left mouse button as you drag the mouse pointer to the right.
	Single word	Position the I-beam pointer on the word and double-click the left mouse button.
	Single sentence	Hold down the `Ctrl` key and click once with the I-beam pointer positioned within the sentence.
	Block of text	Move the cursor to the beginning of the block of text, and then position the I-beam pointer at the end of the block. Hold down the `Shift` key and click once.
	Single line	Move the mouse pointer into the Selection area, beside the desired line. Wait until the pointer changes to a right-pointing arrow and then click once.
	Single paragraph	Move the mouse pointer into the Selection area, beside the desired paragraph. Wait until the pointer changes to a right-pointing arrow, and double-click.
	Entire document	Move the mouse pointer into the Selection area. Wait until the pointer changes to a right-pointing arrow and then hold down the `Ctrl` key and click once.

To practice moving around a document and selecting text, perform the following steps in the PRACTICE.WRI document.

1. To select a word, position the mouse pointer over the word *concept* in the first sentence and then do the following:
   DOUBLE-CLICK: left mouse button on the word *concept*

2. To select the entire last sentence in the paragraph, position the mouse pointer over any word in the last sentence.

3. PRESS: [Ctrl] and hold it down
   CLICK: left mouse button once
   The entire sentence is selected.

4. To select the first line in the practice paragraph, position the mouse pointer in the Selection area next to the first line (starting with "For.") When the I-beam mouse pointer changes to a pointer:
   CLICK: left mouse button once

5. To delete the selected block of text:
   PRESS: [Delete]
   The highlighted block of text disappears and the remaining text flows in the paragraph to compensate for the missing line.

6. To reverse the last command:
   CHOOSE: Edit, Undo
   The text reappears in the first line.

Quick Reference • CHOOSE: Edit, Undo, or
Undo a Command • PRESS: [Ctrl]+z

FORMATTING TEXT

Formatting a document refers to applying character, paragraph, and document formatting options to text. This section describes and illustrates these three formatting options.

CHARACTER FORMATTING   Enhancing text is referred to as character formatting. Specifically, character formatting involves selecting typefaces, font sizes, and styles for text. Some of the styles available in Write include bold, italic, underline, superscript, and subscript. Write's character formatting commands are accessed through the Character menu option.

When a formatting style is active, a check mark appears beside the command on the pull-down menu.

PARAGRAPH FORMATTING   Paragraph formatting involves changing indentation, alignment, line spacing, and tab settings for a paragraph. Paragraph and document formatting commands are accessible from the Paragraph menu option and from a special document tool called the Ruler. To display the Ruler, you choose the Document, Ruler On command from the menu. When the Ruler is displayed, the command becomes Document, Ruler Off on the pull-down menu. Using a mouse, you can easily indent paragraphs, set tab stops, and change the margins by dragging symbols on the Ruler line. The Ruler buttons, described in Table 3.2, provide quick access to all the commands found on the Paragraph menu.

Table 3.2	*Name*	*Button*	*Description*
Ruler Buttons	Left tab	[t]	Positions a left-aligned tab stop on the Ruler
	Decimal tab	[t.]	Positions a decimal tab on the Ruler for aligning numbers and right aligning text
	Single space	[=]	Single-spaces the selected paragraph
	1.5-line-space	[=]	Spaces the selected paragraph by 1.5 lines
	Double space	[=]	Double-spaces the selected paragraph
	Left align	[≡]	Aligns text at the left margin but provides jagged right edges as a typewriter does
	Center align	[≡]	Centers the line or paragraph between the left and right margins
	Right align	[≡]	Positions text flush with the right margin
	Justify	[≡]	Aligns text at the left and right margins, similar to the paragraphs in this guide

DOCUMENT FORMATTING   Document formatting refers to the creation, insertion, and modification of headers, footers, page numbers, and margins in a document. A document **header** and **footer** can appear at the top and bottom of each page. The header often contains the title or heading for a document while the footer shows the page numbers. You choose the Document, Header command or the Document, Footer command to create a header or a footer for a document. The Document, Page Layout command enables you to specify the top, bottom, left, and right margins for the printed document.

Perform the following steps to practice the character, paragraph, and document formatting commands.

1. Ensure that PRACTICE.WRI appears in the Write document window.

2. To practice enhancing text, select the word "difficult" in the first sentence and then do the following:
   CHOOSE: Character, Bold
   The selection is made bold and the text remains highlighted.

3. To italicize the same word using a keyboard shortcut:
   PRESS: Ctrl+i
   The selection is now italicized and bold.

4. To underline the word "traditional" in the second sentence, select the text and then do the following:
   CHOOSE: Character, Underline

5. To make the heading text "Word Processing" bold and underlined, select the text and then do the following:
   PRESS: Ctrl+b
   PRESS: Ctrl+u

6. To center the heading text:
   CHOOSE: Paragraph, Centered
   The heading is centered between the margins.

7. Position the cursor anywhere in the paragraph.

8. CHOOSE: Document, Ruler On

9. CLICK: Justify button in the Ruler (see Table 3.2)

10. To modify the margin settings for the document:
    CHOOSE: Document, Page Layout

11. Set the left and right margins to 1.5 inches:
    PRESS: Tab
    TYPE: 1.5
    PRESS: Tab
    TYPE: 1.5
    PRESS: Enter or CLICK: OK
    Notice that the symbols on the Ruler line have moved to show the new margin settings.

12. Save the document and overwrite the existing version:
    CHOOSE: File, Save
    Your screen should now appear similar to Figure 3.3.

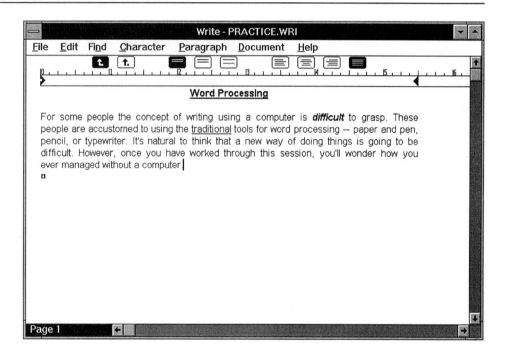

Figure 3.3

Formatting the PRACTICE.WRI document

Quick Reference Character Formatting	1. SELECT: *desired text for formatting* 2. CHOOSE: Character, *command*

Quick Reference Paragraph Formatting	1. Position the cursor in the paragraph to be formatted, or select several paragraphs using the mouse or keyboard. 2. CHOOSE: Paragraph, *command*, or CLICK: *the appropriate symbol in the Ruler*

Quick Reference	• CHOOSE: Document, Header to create a header
Document	• CHOOSE: Document, Footer to create a footer
Formatting	• CHOOSE: Document, Page Layout to specify the margin settings

PRINTING A DOCUMENT

Before you send a document to the printer, choose the File, Repaginate command to have Write finalize the page breaks and renumber the pages. When you are ready to print the document, choose the File, Print command to display the following dialog box:

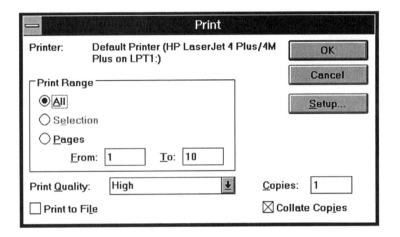

Let's print the practice paragraph.

1. To print the practice paragraph:
   CHOOSE: File, Print
   Because the document is only one paragraph in length, you don't need to repaginate the file before printing.

2. Ensure that the All option is selected in the Print Range area.

3. PRESS: [Enter] or CLICK: OK
   The document is sent to the printer.

Quick Reference	1. CHOOSE: File, Print
Printing a	2. Specify what to print in the Print Range area.
Document	3. PRESS: [Enter] or CLICK: OK

LEAVING WRITE

When you are finished using Windows Write, save your work and exit the program. Perform the following steps.

1. To exit Write:
   CHOOSE: File, Exit

2. If you have made modifications to the current document, a dialog box appears. To abort the modifications and exit:
   SELECT: No

Quick Reference
Exiting Write

1. CHOOSE: File, Exit
2. If necessary, respond to the prompts for saving or aborting the current document, or cancel the command altogether.

USING PAINTBRUSH

The Paintbrush accessory program enables you to create, modify, and save graphic pictures, including drawings, scanned images, and screen captures. You can print these graphics directly from Paintbrush or you can paste them into documents created using other applications, such as Word or PageMaker. To load Paintbrush and display a blank canvas, you double-click the Paintbrush program icon in the Accessories group window.

The Paintbrush application window (Figure 3.4) consists of the following components: Tool Box, Line Width Area, Color Palette, and Canvas. The Tool Box contains icons for drawing and filling shapes, typing text, erasing elements, and moving parts of a drawing. The Line Width Area lets you change the width of all tools that produce lines. In a color picture, Paintbrush provides a color palette. In a monochrome picture, Paintbrush provides a pattern palette. You choose a foreground color/pattern by pointing at the desired option and clicking the left mouse button. You select a background color/pattern by pointing at the desired option and clicking the right mouse button.

Figure 3.4

The Paintbrush application window

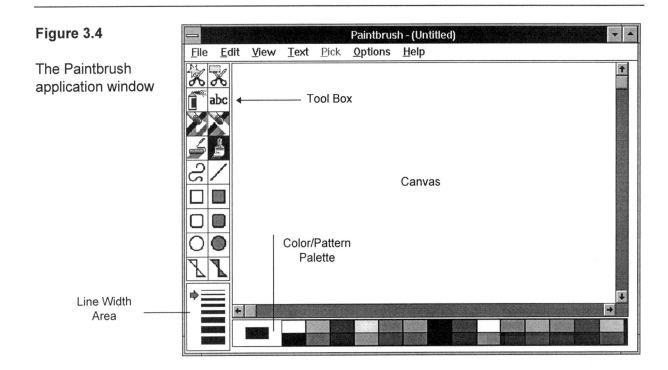

When you first load Paintbrush, the Brush tool is chosen by default. To change the selected tool, you click on the desired icon in the Tool Box. Table 3.3 provides a description of all the tools in the Tool Box.

Table 3.3

Tool Box icons

Name	Icon	Description
Scissors		Selects a freehand area of the drawing
Pick		Selects a rectangular area of the drawing
Airbrush		Spray-paints the current color onto the canvas
Text tool	abc	Enters text
Color Eraser		Erases text or graphics of the selected color
Eraser		Erases all text or graphics regardless of color
Paint Roller		Fills a shape with the currently selected color
Brush		Draws with the current color

Table 3.3 (Continued)	Name	Icon	Description
	Curve		Creates a curved line
	Line		Draws a straight line
	Box		Draws an empty box
	Filled Box		Draws a box filled with the current color
	Round Box		Draws an empty box with rounded edges
	Filled Round Box		Draws a filled box with rounded edges
	Ellipse		Draws an empty circle or ellipse
	Filled Ellipse		Draws an ellipse filled with the current color
	Polygon		Draws an empty polygon
	Filled Polygon		Draws a polygon filled with the current color

Perform the following steps to create the map that appears in Figure 3.5.

Figure 3.5

Drawing a map using Paintbrush

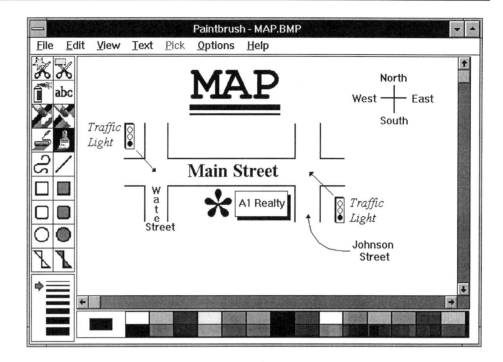

1. Open the Accessories group window and double-click the Paintbrush program icon.

2. To draw Main Street, use the Line tool:
   CLICK: Line tool

3. Position the cross hair on the canvas at the west end of the road.

4. CLICK: left mouse button and hold it down
   DRAG: cross-hair mouse pointer to the east end of the road

5. Release the mouse button to complete the line.

6. Using the same steps that you used to create the initial line, use the Line, Box, Filled Box, Circle, Filled Circle, Text, and Eraser tools to complete the rest of the map.

7. To save the map:
   CHOOSE: File, Save As
   TYPE: a:map
   PRESS: [Enter] or CLICK: OK

8. Exit Paintbrush.

Learning to create a graphic takes many hours of practice and much patience. For more information on Paintbrush, choose the Help option in the menu.

USING OTHER ACCESSORIES

This section introduces several accessories that you can explore on your own time. To load these programs, you open the Accessories group and then double-click the appropriate program icon. In the next section, you learn to use Windows' multitasking capability in an exercise that applies some of the accessories discussed below.

CALCULATOR   The Windows Calculator provides both a general and scientific version of a standard desktop calculator. You use Calculator to perform quick calculations while working in other application programs. For example, you could use Calculator to multiply an invoice amount by a tax rate when creating an invoice in Write. The results of any calculation can be copied to the Windows Clipboard for pasting into other documents or applications.

CALENDAR   Windows provides you with a Calendar program for maintaining an on-line appointment book. When you select the Calendar program icon in the Accessories group window, an empty appointment calendar appears. You can use this calendar to enter new appointments or retrieve a calendar file that you have previously saved to a disk. As in a normal appointment book, you enter information in the appropriate time slots. At the bottom of the window, Calendar provides a scratch pad that you can use to enter notes or reminders while working in the diary. In the application window, you can display either a daily appointment book or a monthly calendar.

CARDFILE   The Cardfile program lets you automate your filing system. It enables you to store and retrieve information, such as phone numbers and recipes, using electronic 3- by 5-inch index cards. In the Cardfile application window, you display information using either the Card view or the List view. The Card view shows all the information for the top index card and layers the remaining cards behind. Each index card consists of an index line at the top of the card and an information area. Cardfile sorts the cards based on your entry in the index line—usually a name. The information area can contain various types of data, including text, pictures, or sound recordings. The List view displays the index line of each card in a report format—perfect for printing out a quick summary of a file. Cardfile displays the current view and number of cards on the Status line, located below the Menu bar.

CLOCK   The Windows Clock program displays the date and time from your computer's internal clock. Clock has two options for displaying the time: analog and digital. When you launch the Clock program from the Accessories window, an analog clock appears on the screen. If you want to display a digital clock face, choose the Settings, Digital command. If you want the current date displayed in the window as well, choose Settings, Date. Other options in the Settings pull-down menu allow you to change the display font, hide the Title bar, or suppress the seconds from being shown. To have the Clock window float above all other open windows (even when it is not the active window), choose the Always on Top command from the Clock's Control menu.

NOTEPAD   As a text editor, the Windows Notepad program does not provide sophisticated word processing capabilities like those available in Windows Write. With Notepad, you create, save, and print batch files (BAT), system files (SYS), and other **ASCII** text files (unformatted files containing characters from the American Standard Code for Information Interchange). It is designed primarily to create simple text files consisting of line item entries.

TERMINAL   The Terminal accessory program enables you to communicate with another computer or a communication service, such as CompuServe. In addition to the Terminal software, you require a **modem** to successfully communicate across telephone lines. For example, if you want to send a file to an associate, you both require modems to complete the file transfer. If your computers reside in the same office, you can connect your computers using a null modem cable instead of a modem. Regardless of the type of hardware used to make the connection, both computers require a software program, such as Terminal, to complete the communication link.

MULTITASKING

With Windows' multitasking capability, you can execute multiple application programs concurrently. Besides saving time, multitasking facilitates the exchange of data among application programs. Information that you cut or copy from an application is placed in a special area of memory called the Clipboard. You can paste the contents of the Clipboard to another location in the same application or to another running application.

Multitasking in Windows is controlled using Task Manager. Task Manager enables you to list running applications, move among them, and close applications. To display Task Manager, press [Ctrl]+[Esc] or double-click on an empty area of the desktop.

To move quickly among running applications, you can bypass Task Manager altogether by holding down the [Alt] key while you press [Tab]. With each press of the [Tab] key, the name of a running application appears on a message board in the middle of the screen. When the desired application appears, you release the [Alt] key to move to that application.

Perform the following steps.

1. Ensure that the Program Manager application window appears.

2. Let's load some of the Windows accessories. After opening the Accessories group window, do the following:
   DOUBLE-CLICK: Cardfile icon
   PRESS: [Alt]+[Tab] to return to the Program Manager
   DOUBLE-CLICK: Paintbrush icon
   PRESS: [Alt]+[Tab] to return to the Program Manager
   DOUBLE-CLICK: Write icon
   PRESS: [Alt]+[Tab] to return to the Program Manager

3. Minimize the Program Manager application window.

4. To call up the Windows Task Manager:
   PRESS: [Ctrl]+[Esc]
   You should have at least the following programs displayed in the task list: Write, Paintbrush, Notepad, and Program Manager.

Session 3

5. To organize the running applications on the desktop:
   CLICK: Cascade command button in Task Manager
   Your screen should appear similar to Figure 3.6.

Figure 3.6

Cascading open application programs

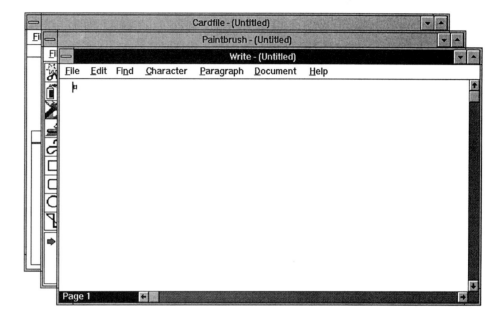

6. Practice moving among the applications using the mouse:
   CLICK: Paintbrush window
   Watch the application Title bars to see which window is active.

7. Practice moving among the applications using the keyboard:
   PRESS: (Alt) and hold it down
   PRESS: (Tab) until Cardfile appears
   Release the (Alt) key.

8. To create a new card in Cardfile, you must first create the index entry:
   CHOOSE: Card, Add
   TYPE: Veiner, Sima
   PRESS: (Enter) or CLICK: OK

9. Let's complete Sima's card:
   TYPE: `Sima Veiner, Product Manager`
   PRESS: [Enter]
   TYPE: `Microsoft Corporation`
   PRESS: [Enter]
   TYPE: `One Microsoft Way`
   PRESS: [Enter]
   TYPE: `Redmond, WA  98052`

10. Using the mouse and dragging the I-beam:
    SELECT: *all the text on the new card under the Index line*

11. To copy this information to the Clipboard:
    CHOOSE: Edit, Copy

12. SELECT: Write application window using [Alt]+[Tab]

13. TYPE: `September 30, 1994`
    PRESS: [Enter] three times

14. CHOOSE: Edit, Paste
    The information is inserted at the current cursor position in Write.

15. To insert some blank lines:
    PRESS: [Enter] twice

16. TYPE: `Dear Sima:`
    PRESS: [Enter] twice
    TYPE: `Thanks for the product information.`
    PRESS: [Enter] twice

17. SELECT: Paintbrush application window

18. Try to sign your name on the canvas:
    DRAG: the Brush tool like a pen

19. SELECT: the Pick tool (✂) from the Tool Box

20. Starting at the top left-hand corner of your signature:
    CLICK: left mouse button and hold it down
    DRAG: mouse pointer to the bottom right-hand corner so that the rectangle surrounds the entire signature
    (*Note*: Do not include too much white space in the selection.)

21. Release the mouse button.

22. Copy the outlined graphic to the Clipboard:
    CHOOSE: Edit, Copy

23. SELECT: Write application window

24. To paste the signature into the Write document:
    CHOOSE: Edit, Paste
    The graphic appears in the document, similar to Figure 3.7.

Figure 3.7

The completed Write document

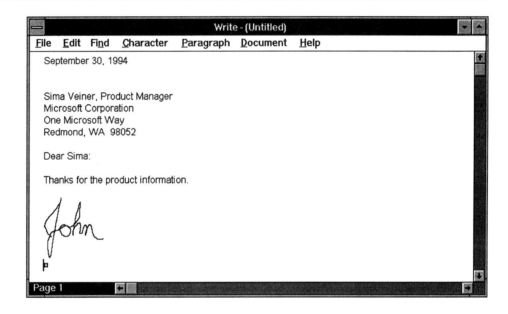

25. To save the Write document:
    CHOOSE: File, Save As
    TYPE: a:ltrhead
    PRESS: [Enter] or CLICK: OK

26. Close all the open applications, except for Program Manager. Do not save the changes when prompted by Windows.

SUMMARY

This session introduced you to some of the tools that accompany the Windows graphical environment. In addition to several system utility programs, Windows provides a feature-rich word processing program called Write, a drawing package called Paintbrush, and the Terminal communications program. There are also four personal productivity programs called Clock, Calculator, Cardfile, and Calendar.

Some of the commands and procedures introduced in this session appear in the Command Summary (Table 3.4).

Table 3.4

Command Summary

Command	Description
File, New	Creates a new document file to use in an application
File, Open	Retrieves a file from the disk to use in an application
File, Save	Saves a document file to permanent storage
File, Save As	Saves a document file under a new name or location
File, Print	Prints a document file
File, Exit	Leaves an application program
Character, *command*	In Write, formats and enhances text using boldface, italic, underlines, and fonts
Paragraph, *command*	In Write, formats a paragraph's alignment and line spacing
Document, *command*	In Write, formats the document using headers and footers; defines page layout options, such as margins

KEY TERMS

ASCII   Acronym for American Standard Code for Information Interchange. An ASCII text file refers to an unformatted text file that is viewed or edited using DOS or the Notepad accessory program.

End mark   The symbol that appears at the end of a Write document. You cannot move the cursor beyond this mark.

footer   Descriptive text that appears at the bottom of each page in a document. The footer usually contains page numbers.

header   Descriptive text that appears at the top of each page in a document. The header usually contains titles or headings.

insertion point   The vertical flashing bar in Write that indicates your current position in the document (also referred to as a cursor). The insertion point shows where the next typed characters will appear.

modem   A device for transferring information between computers using telephone lines; translates digital signals from a computer into analog signals for transmission and then back into digital signals again for processing. (A modem must be hooked up at each end of the transmission.) Modem stands for MOdulate/DEModulate.

Selection area   The leftmost column in the Write document window. The Selection area provides shortcut methods for selecting text using the mouse.

word wrap   When the cursor reaches the right-hand margin of a line, it automatically wraps to the left margin of the next line; the user does not have to press a carriage return key at the end of each line to move the cursor down.

EXERCISES

SHORT ANSWER

1. What is *multimedia*?
2. In Write, what is the Selection area?
3. What are the three levels of formatting in Write?
4. How does the Ruler assist you in formatting a document?
5. In Write, what should you do before sending a multiple-page document to the printer?
6. What are the four main components of the Paintbrush screen?
7. Name two methods for connecting computers in order to transfer files.
8. How can you keep the Clock from being overlaid by other application windows on the desktop?
9. What two views are provided in the Calculator accessory program?
10. How does the Notepad accessory program differ from Write?

HANDS-ON

(*Note*: In the following exercises, you perform Windows commands using files located on the Advantage Diskette.)

1. Using the Write word processing program, create the document appearing in Figure 3.8. Make sure to include your name in the closing of the letter. Save this document onto the Advantage Diskette as LETTER.

Figure 3.8

LETTER
document

August 28, 1994

Ms. Juanita Pallos
2910 S.W. Marine Drive
Suite 1201
Stanford, CA 94305

Dear Ms. Pallos:

Thank you for your letter regarding the upcoming event. I am in complete agreement with you that the number of persons attending must be limited to 350. In addition, your idea of having this event catered sounds fantastic.

Moving to a different subject, I noticed that the letter you wrote me was typed using a typewriter. With the number of letters you write, you really should consider purchasing a microcomputer and word processing software program.

If you are interested, I would be happy to show you some word processing fundamentals. We could even use my computer to design and print the invitations for the event!

Best regards,

your name

a. Insert the following text between the second and third paragraphs:

   Specifically, word processing software makes it easier to change a document by allowing you to:

   1.   Insert text
   2.   Delete text

```
       3.   Copy and move text
       4.   Format text
```

    b. In the first line of the last paragraph, delete the words "If you are interested," and start the sentence with "If you can spare the time."
    c. Save the document back to the Advantage Diskette as NEWLET.
    d. Print the document.
    e. Quit Write.

2. Using Cardfile, create and save a file on the Advantage Diskette called CLIENTS that contains the information provided below. Each row in the table should be placed onto a separate card.
    a. Sort the cards according to the client's surname. (*Hint*: A card file is sorted by the information appearing in the index line.)
    b. Print two reports: a summary list and the complete card information.

Given	Surname	Address	City	State	Zip
Elliot	Lepinski	898 Burrard Avenue	Louisville	KY	40205
Red	Robinson	235 Johnson Street	Washington	DC	20052
Elaine	Maynard	1005 West 9th Street, #705	Baton Rouge	LA	70803
Ranjitt	Singh	1227 E. Cordova Avenue	Tacoma	WA	98416
William	Delaney	36 Primore Road	Wichita	KS	67208
Francisco	Ortez	875 Broadway	Albuquerque	NM	87131
Alice	Chan	29 Redmond Road	San Francisco	CA	92182
Jessica	Thomas	909 West 18th Street, #12	Brooklyn	NY	11225
Jimmy	Kazo	888 East 8th Avenue	Billings	MT	59101
Kelly	Judson	1984 Orwell Road	Tacoma	WA	98405
Paul	Mang	12555 Horseshoe Way	Washington	DC	20055
Wanda	Roo	Building C, 10 Main St.	Brooklyn	NY	11230

SESSION 4

SIMPLY WINDOWS: MANAGING YOUR WORK

For the same reasons you arrange folders in a filing cabinet or organize your desk, you use directories to manage your work on disks. With the Windows File Manager, you can perform routine disk, directory, and file management tasks, such as formatting diskettes, creating directories, copying files, or deleting an entire disk's contents.

PREVIEW

When you have completed this session, you will be able to:

Explain the importance of a directory structure.

-

Load File Manager.

-

Customize and work with directory windows.

-

Copy, move, rename, and delete files.

-

Create a directory structure.

-

Work with subdirectories.

Session Outline

Why This Session Is Important
What Is File Management?
What Is Disk Management?
File- and Disk-Naming Conventions
Using File Manager
    The Guided Tour
    Customizing the Directory Window
    Selecting Drives
    Selecting Files
Managing Files
    Customizing the Directory Contents Pane
    Working with Multiple Directory Windows
    Copying and Moving Files
    Renaming Files
    Deleting Files
Managing Disks and Directories
    Creating a Directory
    Selecting a Directory
    Copying and Moving Files to Subdirectories
    Removing a Directory
    Renaming a Directory
    Preparing New Disks
Summary
    Command Summary
Key Terms
Exercises
    Short Answer
    Hands-On

Session 4

WHY THIS SESSION IS IMPORTANT

This session introduces the procedures for managing your files and disks in Windows. File management involves copying, moving, renaming, and deleting individual files and groups of files. Directory or disk management focuses on creating and working with directory structures on hard disks and floppy diskettes, rather than with the individual files on those disks. In this session, you perform a variety of file and disk management tasks using the Windows File Manager.

Before proceeding, make sure the following are true:

1. You have turned on your computer system and loaded Windows 3.1.
2. The Program Manager window appears on the screen.
3. Your Advantage Diskette is inserted into drive A:. You will work with files on the diskette that have been created for you. (*Note*: The Advantage Diskette can be duplicated by copying all of the files from your instructor's Master Advantage Diskette.)

WHAT IS FILE MANAGEMENT?

File management is the process of managing the work that you create and store on hard disks and floppy diskettes. Each document that you create is stored in a disk file, similar to a file folder in a manual filing system. Managing your work involves copying, renaming, and deleting files.

There are three categories of files that appear on hard disks and floppy diskettes: program files, document files, and data files. **Program files** consist of computer instructions for performing a certain task or for running an application software program. **Document files** contain work that you create using an application program recognized by Windows. Those documents for which Windows does not recognize the files' types are called **data files**. The file management principles discussed in this session apply equally to program, document, and data files.

WHAT IS DISK MANAGEMENT?

Disk management is the process of managing the storage areas in your computer. These storage areas can be vast. For example, one hard disk can store data that would normally fill several large filing cabinets. On a new disk, there is only one area for storing files: the **root directory**. From the root directory, you create additional storage areas called **subdirectories**.

Think of the root directory as the top of a filing cabinet and each subdirectory as a drawer or folder in the cabinet. If you continually placed documents on top of the cabinet, the files would quickly reach the ceiling. One solution would be to move the files from the top of the filing cabinet into the cabinet drawers. On a computer, you move files from the root directory to subdirectories on the hard disk. You can also create subdirectories within subdirectories. The organization of subdirectories is called a **directory structure** or **directory tree**.

In addition to creating directory structures, disk management involves preparing new disks for storing data and labeling disks.

FILE- AND DISK-NAMING CONVENTIONS

Before you perform file and disk management operations, you should understand the following DOS rules for naming files and disk drives:

1. A complete filename consists of a file name and an extension, separated by a period (for example, FILENAME.EXT). Every disk file must have a name; the extension, however, is optional. The name of a file reflects its content, while the extension commonly indicates the application software program used to create the file.

2. A file name can contain one to eight characters, with no spaces.

3. An **extension** can contain up to three characters, with no spaces.

4. Although you can use some special symbols in a file name, such as the ampersand (&) or underscore (_), try to use only letters and numbers. You must avoid symbols that DOS reserves for its own commands, for example, *, ?, |, <, >.

There are several possible disk drive configurations for microcomputers and knowing how to reference each storage area is crucial to working with DOS and Windows. The first diskette drive is always referred to as drive A:. If your computer has two diskette drives, drive A: is usually positioned to the left or above the second diskette drive, called drive B:. If your computer has a hard disk drive, it is referred to as drive C:. The drive letter is always followed by a colon (:) to represent a drive designation.

USING FILE MANAGER

With File Manager you are able to perform most DOS management tasks using Windows' menu-driven visual interface. Accessed from the Main group window in Program Manager, File Manager provides a graphical view of a disk's directory structure and its files.

Perform the following steps.

1. Ensure that the Program Manager window is displayed.

2. Open the Main group window.

3. DOUBLE-CLICK: File Manager icon ()
   Your screen should now appear similar to Figure 4.1. (*Note*: The files and directories stored in your computer will differ from those in Figure 4.1. As well, the screen graphic shows the File Manager program that is provided with Windows for Workgroups 3.11, which differs slightly from the version included in Windows 3.1.)

Figure 4.1

File Manager application window

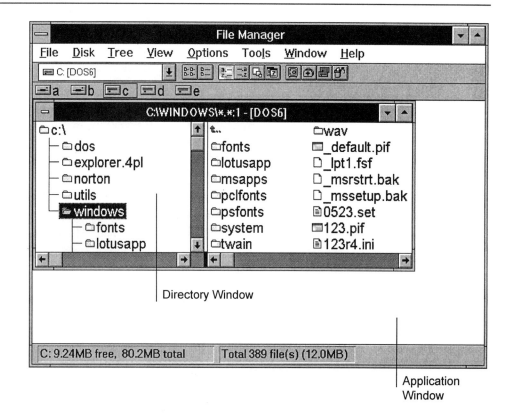

| Quick Reference | 1. Open the Main group window in the Program Manager window. |
| Loading File Manager | 2. DOUBLE-CLICK: File Manager icon |

THE GUIDED TOUR

When you first load File Manager, a single **directory window** appears in the application window. Directory windows display the directory structure and contents of disk drives. To facilitate managing files on various drives, you can open several directory windows simultaneously in the application window. You can also move, size, and arrange directory windows within File Manager to best suit your needs and available work space.

At the top of the application window, File Manager provides a menu for choosing file and disk management commands. In Windows for Workgroups 3.11, File Manager displays a Tool bar and the drive icons beneath the Menu bar. The Status bar at the bottom of the application window displays information for the selected disk drive and highlighted directory. The left side of the Status bar shows the available space and total capacity of the drive. The right side of the Status bar shows the number of files in the directory, along with their accumulated size.

Session 4

The directory window is divided into two panes by a vertical line called the **Split bar**. The left pane contains a graphical depiction of the directory tree for the selected disk drive. The right pane displays the contents of the highlighted folder in the directory tree. As explained later in this session, you can move the Split bar to increase or decrease the viewing area in either pane. Other important components of a directory window are shown in Figure 4.2, including the directory path, directory icons, file icons, scroll bars, Split bar, and **Selection cursor**.

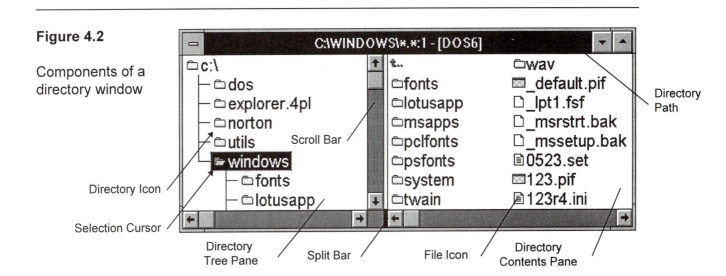

Figure 4.2

Components of a directory window

To work most efficiently with a directory window, you manipulate its icons using a mouse. Table 4.1 describes the components in a directory window.

Table 4.1

Explanation of the Components in a Directory Window

Component	Description
Directory path	The directory window Title bar contains the **file specification**, including the current directory path. The *.* **wildcard character** specification displays all files in the selected directory.
Directory icons (🗀)	A folder icon represents a directory or subdirectory.

Table 4.1
Continued

Component	Description
Program file icon (▢)	A program file icon represents a program or batch file. A program file typically has one of the following extensions: COM, EXE, PIF, or BAT.
Document file icon (▤)	A document file icon represents a data file that is associated with an application.
Data file icon (▯)	A data file icon represents a file that is not associated with an application.
Up icon (📁)	In the directory contents pane, select the Up icon to move to the previous level or directory.
Split bar	You use the mouse to drag the Split bar in order to size the panes in the directory window.
Scroll bars	Scroll bars facilitate moving through the tree pane and directory contents pane using a mouse.
Selection cursor	You use the Selection cursor to select a drive icon, directory folder icon, or file icon.

CUSTOMIZING THE DIRECTORY WINDOW

A directory window initially displays the directory tree pane and the directory contents pane. You can also customize the display to view a single pane in the directory window using the View menu option. Rather than splitting the directory window equally between the panes, you can adjust the area using the Split bar.

Perform the following steps to customize your directory window.

1. To display the directory tree only in the directory window:
   CHOOSE: View, Tree Only
   Notice that the active option in the pull-down menu has a check mark beside the command.

2. To display the directory contents only in the directory window:
   CHOOSE: View, Directory Only

Session 4

3. To display both the directory tree pane and directory contents pane:
   CHOOSE: View, Tree and Directory

Quick Reference
Customizing the Directory Window

- CHOOSE: View, Tree Only to view the directory tree pane only
- CHOOSE: View, Directory Only to view the contents pane only
- CHOOSE: View, Tree and Directory to view both panes

SELECTING DRIVES

To display the directory tree and files for a disk drive, you select the drive using the keyboard or a mouse. Using the keyboard, you select a drive by pressing and holding down the [Ctrl] key and then tapping the desired drive letter. For example, [Ctrl]+c selects drive C: and [Ctrl]+a selects drive A:. Using a mouse, you click once on the desired drive icon.

Perform the following steps.

1. Ensure that the Advantage Diskette is placed into drive A:.

2. To view the directory tree and files on drive A:, do the following:
   PRESS: [Ctrl]+a

3. To view the directory tree and files on drive C:, do the following:
   CLICK: drive C: icon (▯c) once

Quick Reference
Selecting a Drive

- PRESS: [Ctrl]+*drive letter*, or
- CLICK: desired drive icon once

SELECTING FILES

File Manager is based on a "Select" and then "Do" philosophy whereby you highlight directories and files and then execute commands from the menu. When you select a directory in the directory tree pane, the subdirectories and files in that directory are displayed in the directory contents pane. Table 4.2 summarizes the methods for selecting files in the directory contents pane.

Table 4.2	*Using the Keyboard*	*Using a Mouse*
Selecting Files	Move the Selection cursor over the file using the cursor-movement keys.	Position the mouse pointer over the file and click the left mouse button once.
Group of Files	PRESS: [Shift]+[↓]	CLICK: first file in the group PRESS: [Shift] and hold it down CLICK: last file in the group
Other Options	To select all the files in the window: PRESS: [Ctrl]+/ (forward slash)	To select a non-contiguous group of files, do the following: CLICK: first file in the group PRESS: [Ctrl] and hold it down CLICK: all additional files in the group

Perform the following steps to practice selecting files.

1. To display files for drive A: sorted by file name:
   PRESS: [Ctrl]+a
   CHOOSE: View, Sort by Name

2. To select the first five files in the directory contents pane:
   CLICK: the first file in the list
   PRESS: [Shift] and hold it down
   CLICK: the fifth file in the list

3. Release the [Shift] key.

4. To select three noncontiguous files:
   PRESS: [Home] to remove the previous selection

5. CLICK: CASH.XLS file once

6. To select the additional files:
   PRESS: [Ctrl] and hold it down

7. CLICK: CLIENTS.DBF
   Notice that the first file in the list remains highlighted.

8. CLICK: ETHICS.WPD

9. Release the [Ctrl] key.

Your screen should now appear similar to Figure 4.3.

Figure 4.3

Selecting multiple files using the mouse

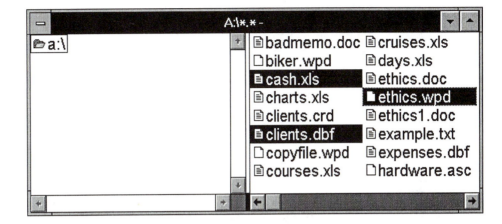

Quick Reference	1. CLICK: the first file to select
Selecting Files	2. PRESS: Ctrl and hold it down
	3. CLICK: each additional file to include in the selection
	4. Release the Ctrl key.

MANAGING FILES

Managing files involves displaying, organizing, selecting, copying, moving, renaming, and deleting files. Although most file management commands are available from the File pull-down menu in File Manager, you can also use keyboard shortcuts and drag and drop mouse techniques.

CUSTOMIZING THE DIRECTORY CONTENTS PANE

Working with the directory contents pane in its default view is sufficient for many users. However, you may want to view additional file statistics, such as the size of a file or when it was last modified. Using the View menu option, you can customize and sort the file information displayed in the directory contents pane.

VIEWING FILE DETAILS   To modify the view for files in the directory contents pane, choose the View command from the menu.

Perform the following steps.

1. Ensure that the directory window displays the A:*.* file specification.

2. To view all the file details in the directory contents pane:
   CHOOSE: View, All File Details

3. Using a mouse, expand the directory window by dragging its borders down and to the right. If you cannot see all the file detail information, reduce the directory tree area by dragging the Split bar to the left. Your screen should appear similar to Figure 4.4.

Figure 4.4

Viewing all file details

Name	Size	Date	Time	
badmemo.doc	10596	9/22/93	12:00:00pm	a
biker.wpd	14744	3/7/94	12:48:00pm	a
cash.xls	6483	11/4/93	10:03:30am	a
charts.xls	4155	11/4/93	11:41:40pm	a
clients.crd	1244	6/5/94	9:22:46pm	a
clients.dbf	2290	11/9/92	10:48:32am	a
copyfile.wpd	3724	9/22/93	12:00:00pm	a
courses.xls	2729	11/4/93	10:04:56am	a
cruises.xls	2097	11/4/93	10:05:18am	a
days.xls	7968	11/4/93	10:06:30am	a
ethics.doc	10340	2/25/94	2:50:12pm	a
ethics.wpd	10058	3/1/94	2:32:44pm	a

Quick Reference
Viewing File Details
- CHOOSE: View, Name to view file names and extensions only
- CHOOSE: View, All File Details to view all the files' statistics

SORTING FILES   To sort the files in the directory contents pane, choose one of the following View commands: Sort by Name, Sort by Type, Sort by Size, or Sort by Date. Most of these sort options are self-explanatory. The active sort order has a check mark appearing beside the command in the View pull-down menu.

Perform the following steps.

1. To sort files according to size in the directory contents window:
   CHOOSE: View, Sort by Size

2. To sort files according to their file name extensions:
   CHOOSE: View, Sort by Type

3. To sort files according to name (the default):
   CHOOSE: View, Sort by Name

4. To view only the names of files in the directory contents pane:
   CHOOSE: View, Name

Quick Reference *Sorting Files in the* *Directory Contents* *Pane*	• CHOOSE: View, Sort by Name to sort files by file name • CHOOSE: View, Sort by Type to sort files by extension • CHOOSE: View, Sort by Size to sort files by size • CHOOSE: View, Sort by Date to sort files by date

WORKING WITH MULTIPLE DIRECTORY WINDOWS

To facilitate copying and moving files among disk drives and directories, File Manager allows you to open multiple directory windows simultaneously. To open a new directory window, you double-click the mouse pointer on a drive icon or choose the Window, New Window command. Similar to organizing group windows in Program Manager, you arrange your open directory windows using the Window, Cascade and Window, Tile commands.

When working with multiple directory windows, you must select the desired window to make it active before issuing a menu command. If a window is hidden from view, choose the Window command and then select the appropriate window from the list on the pull-down menu.

Perform the following steps to practice working with multiple windows.

1. Ensure that the directory window displays A:*.* in its Title bar.

2. To open a new window:
   CHOOSE: Window, New Window
   Notice that each directory window Title bar has a number attached to the A:*.* file specification for identification.

3. To open a new window for drive C:, do the following:
   DOUBLE-CLICK: drive C: icon (🖴c)

CAUTION: If you single-click the drive C: icon by mistake, the active window changes its display to show files and directories for drive C:. When you double-click the icon, a third window should appear.

4. To tile the open directory windows:
   CHOOSE: Window, Tile
   (*Note*: If you are using Windows for Workgroups, choose Window, Tile, Horizontally.) Your screen should appear similar to Figure 4.5.

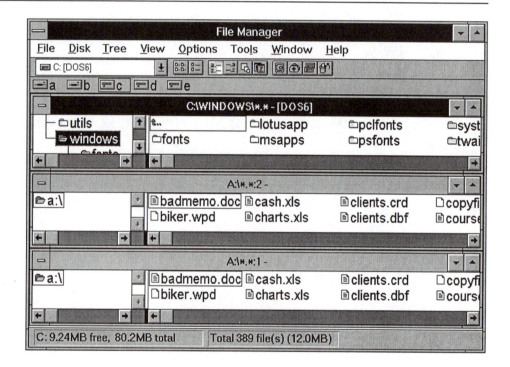

Figure 4.5

Using the Window, Tile command

5. To cascade the windows:
   CHOOSE: Window, Cascade
   The windows are layered in the application window.

6. To close the drive C: window:
   DOUBLE-CLICK: Control menu for the drive C: directory window

7. Close the A:*.*:2 window.

8. To update the information in the remaining directory window:
   CHOOSE: Window, Refresh
   The Title bar now reads A:*.* for the directory window.

Quick Reference *Opening a New Directory Window*	• CHOOSE: <u>W</u>indow, <u>N</u>ew Window, or • DOUBLE-CLICK: the desired drive's icon

COPYING AND MOVING FILES

The standard method for copying and moving files using File Manager is to first select the desired files and then to issue either the <u>F</u>ile, <u>C</u>opy or <u>F</u>ile, <u>M</u>ove command. A better and faster method is to use **drag and drop**. Using the mouse, you can copy and move files by dragging them to their new location (for example, a folder in the directory tree pane or an icon in the drive icons area). If you drag files to a different directory on the same drive, Windows executes a Move command. If you drag files to a different drive, Windows executes a <u>C</u>opy command.

Perform the following steps.

1. To display two directory windows:
   CHOOSE: <u>W</u>indow, <u>N</u>ew Window
   CHOOSE: <u>W</u>indow, <u>T</u>ile

2. Display the files for drive A: in the top window and the files for drive C: in the bottom window.

3. CLICK: top folder icon (C:\) in the drive C: directory tree pane
   Your screen should appear similar to Figure 4.6 before continuing. (*Note*: Your screen display will show different file names for drive C: than the screen graphic in Figure 4.6.)

Figure 4.6

Viewing files from drive A: and drive C: at the same time

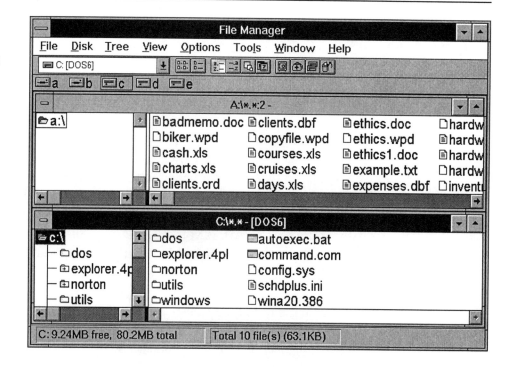

4. To copy multiple files using the drag and drop method, first select the files in the top directory window (A:*.*) using the mouse:
   CLICK: BADMEMO.DOC
   PRESS: Ctrl and hold it down
   CLICK: DAYS.XLS
   CLICK: EXPENSES.DBF

5. Release the Ctrl key. The files remain highlighted in reverse video.

6. Position the mouse pointer over one of the highlighted files.

7. CLICK: left mouse button and hold it down

8. DRAG: mouse pointer to the root directory folder in drive C:
   Position the mouse pointer directly over the top folder appearing in the directory tree pane for drive C:. (*Note*: You can also drop the files on the drive C: icon in the drive icons area. However, the files are copied or moved to the default directory on the drive, which may not be the desired directory. Therefore, you should drop files on the target directory folder in the directory tree pane, rather than on a drive icon.)

9. Release the mouse button.

Session 4

10. If the mouse pointer was positioned correctly, a dialog box appears asking you for confirmation to copy the files to drive C:. Answer yes:
    PRESS: [Enter] or CLICK: Yes

    CAUTION: Ensure that the wording in the dialog box is correct before responding to the prompt. Check that the dialog box confirms the Copy or Move command and that the target location is accurate. There is not an Undo command available in the File Manager.

11. To rename a file:
    SELECT: the directory contents pane for drive C:

12. SELECT: DAYS.XLS file
    Make certain that you are selecting the file from the directory contents pane for drive C:, and not drive A:.

13. To rename the file to DAYS.OLD:
    CHOOSE: File, Rename

14. Enter the new name in the dialog box:
    TYPE: days.old
    PRESS: [Enter] or CLICK: OK
    The new file name appears in the directory contents pane.

Quick Reference *Copying and Moving Files*	1. SELECT: the files to copy or move 2. Dragging a file or files between disk drives is a copy operation. 3. Dragging a file or files between directories on the same disk drive represents a move operation. 4. PRESS: [Enter] or CLICK: OK

Quick Reference *Renaming Files*	1. SELECT: the file or files to rename 2. CHOOSE: File, Rename 3. TYPE: new name into the dialog box 4. PRESS: [Enter] or CLICK: OK

DELETING FILES

To delete files using File Manager, you first select the files and then issue the File, Delete command or press [Delete]. When prompted by the dialog box, you confirm each deletion by pressing [Enter] or clicking the Yes command button.

To practice deleting files, perform the following steps.

1. SELECT: the directory contents pane for drive C:

2. SELECT: BADMEMO.DOC file in drive C:

3. To delete the file:
   CHOOSE: File, Delete
   PRESS: [Enter] or CLICK: OK to proceed with the deletion
   PRESS: [Enter] or CLICK: Yes to confirm the deletion

4. To delete several files at once, you first select all the files:
   CLICK: DAYS.OLD
   PRESS: [Ctrl] and hold it down
   CLICK: EXPENSES.DBF

5. Release the [Ctrl] key.

6. To delete the selected files:
   PRESS: [Delete]
   The file names of the selected files appear in the dialog box.

7. When prompted, proceed with the deletion:
   PRESS: [Enter] or CLICK: OK
   CLICK: Yes to All
   The Yes to All command confirms the deletion of all selected files.

8. To close the directory window, do the following:
   DOUBLE-CLICK: Control menu for the drive C: directory window

---

Quick Reference
Deleting Files

1. SELECT: the file or files to delete
2. CHOOSE: File, Delete or PRESS: [Delete]
3. PRESS: [Enter] or CLICK: OK
4. PRESS: [Enter] a second time or CLICK: Yes to confirm

MANAGING DISKS AND DIRECTORIES

File Manager eases the task of directory and disk management. The directory window displays the directory structure for the current disk drive, with the folder icons representing the individual subdirectories. To change the current directory, you select the desired folder icon in the directory tree pane. To create, rename, and remove subdirectories, you issue commands from the File Manager menu.

CREATING A DIRECTORY

You create a directory using the File, Create Directory command from the menu. Before you issue the command, you must select the **parent directory** in the directory tree pane. On a blank disk, the parent directory is always the root directory or top folder icon in the tree structure.

Let's practice creating subdirectories on the Advantage Diskette.

1. Ensure that the directory window displays the A:*.* file specification with both panes visible.

2. CHOOSE: Window, Tile

3. To select the root directory of drive A:, do the following:
   CLICK: directory folder icon in the directory tree pane

4. To create a new subdirectory under the root called WORDDATA:
   CHOOSE: File, Create Directory
   A dialog box appears for you to type the name of the new directory.

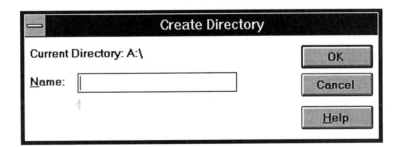

5. To create the WORDDATA directory on drive A:, do the following:
   TYPE: worddata
   PRESS: (Enter)
   Notice that a new **branch** is created in the directory tree pane.

6. To create a new directory under the root called XLDATA:
   CHOOSE: File, Create Directory
   TYPE: xldata
   PRESS: (Enter)

7. You can also create directories within directories. To demonstrate, first select the WORDDATA directory:
   CLICK: WORDDATA directory folder icon
   No files or subdirectories appear in the directory contents pane.

8. To create a subdirectory called LETTERS under WORDDATA:
   CHOOSE: File, Create Directory
   TYPE: letters
   PRESS: (Enter)
   Because LETTERS is a subdirectory of WORDDATA, it is attached to the WORDDATA folder icon in the directory tree pane. The root directory (a:\) is the parent directory of WORDDATA, and WORDDATA is the parent directory of LETTERS.

9. To create another subdirectory under the WORDDATA directory:
   CHOOSE: File, Create Directory
   TYPE: memos
   PRESS: (Enter)
   Notice that there are now two directory folder icons under WORDDATA—one for LETTERS and one for MEMOS.

10. SELECT: a:\ root directory folder icon
    Your screen should now appear similar to Figure 4.7.

Figure 4.7

The directory tree pane after creating directories

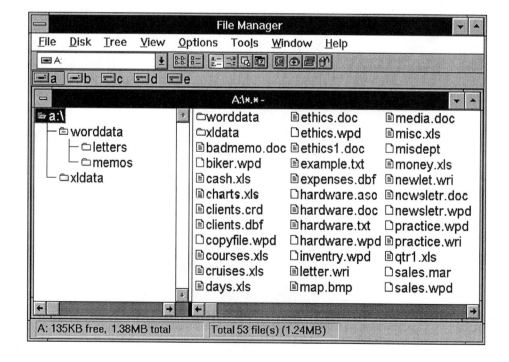

Quick Reference	1. SELECT: parent directory in the directory tree pane
Creating a New Subdirectory	2. CHOOSE: File, Create Directory
	3. TYPE: *name of the new subdirectory*
	4. PRESS: [Enter] or CLICK: OK

SELECTING A DIRECTORY

To move to a different directory in the directory tree pane, you use the keyboard or the mouse. When you select a folder, the files within the directory are displayed in the directory contents pane. However, not all subdirectories are always displayed in the directory tree pane.

The directory tree pane is similar to an outline in which you expand or collapse topics to view more or less detail. If a directory contains subdirectories that are not currently displayed in the tree diagram, a plus sign (+) appears in the parent directory folder. A minus sign (–) in a parent directory folder tells you that all subdirectories are displayed. To display the plus and minus signs in the folder icons, you must choose the Tree, Indicate Expandable Branches command from the menu.

To practice expanding and collapsing the directory tree diagram, perform the following steps.

1. Ensure that a check mark appears next to the Indicate Expandable Branches command in the Tree pull-down menu:
   CHOOSE: Tree, Indicate Expandable Branches

2. SELECT: WORDDATA branch in the directory tree pane
   Notice that the folder has a minus sign (–).

3. To collapse the WORDDATA branch using the mouse:
   DOUBLE-CLICK: – sign on the WORDDATA directory folder icon

4. To collapse the entire directory diagram using the menu:
   SELECT: 📂 a:\ root directory folder icon
   CHOOSE: Tree, Collapse Branch

5. To expand the entire directory tree diagram using the menu:
   CHOOSE: Tree, Expand All

COPYING AND MOVING FILES TO SUBDIRECTORIES

Copying and moving files among subdirectories is identical to copying and moving files between drives. You select the files that you want to copy or move and then you issue the appropriate command. As demonstrated in the following example, moving files into different directories on the same drive is easy using the drag and drop method.

To practice moving a file to a new directory, perform the following steps.

1. To move files from one directory into another, you must first select the source folder in the directory tree pane:
   SELECT: 📁 a:\
   The files in the root directory appear in the directory contents pane.

2. To move a file from the root directory to the LETTERS subdirectory:
   SELECT: HARDWARE.ASC file in the directory contents pane

3. Position the mouse pointer over the selected file.

4. CLICK: left mouse button and hold down
   DRAG: mouse pointer over the LETTERS directory folder icon in the directory tree pane

5. When the mouse pointer is positioned directly on top of the LETTERS folder, the Selection cursor outlines the directory folder. Release the left mouse button.

6. To complete the move operation, respond affirmatively to the confirmation dialog box:
   PRESS: [Enter] or CLICK: Yes

REMOVING A DIRECTORY

You remove a subdirectory using the File, Delete command or the [Delete] key. Make sure that you position the Selection cursor on the subdirectory folder before issuing the Delete command. Perform the following steps.

1. To remove the XLDATA directory:
   SELECT: XLDATA folder icon in the directory tree pane

2. CHOOSE: File, Delete
   PRESS: [Enter] or CLICK: OK

Session 4 103

3. To confirm the directory deletion:
   PRESS: [Enter] or CLICK: Yes

4. To remove the MEMOS directory:
   SELECT: MEMOS folder in the directory tree pane
   PRESS: [Delete]
   PRESS: [Enter] or CLICK: OK to proceed with the deletion
   PRESS: [Enter] or CLICK: Yes to confirm the deletion

5. To remove the LETTERS directory:
   SELECT: LETTERS folder
   PRESS: [Delete]
   PRESS: [Enter] or CLICK: OK to proceed with the deletion
   PRESS: [Enter] or CLICK: Yes to confirm the directory deletion
   PRESS: [Enter] or CLICK: Yes to confirm the file deletion

Quick Reference *Removing a Subdirectory*	1. SELECT: subdirectory to remove in the directory tree pane 2. CHOOSE: File, Delete, or PRESS: [Delete] 3. PRESS: [Enter] or CLICK: OK 4. PRESS: [Enter] or CLICK: Yes to confirm

RENAMING A DIRECTORY

The File, Rename command allows you to rename both files and directories. Like most commands in File Manager, you must first select the directory that you want renamed before issuing the command. Once the command is executed, you complete the following dialog box (as shown in the following example):

```
┌─────────────────────────── Rename ───────────────────────────┐
│ Current Directory: A:\                          ┌────────┐   │
│ From:    [WORDDATA        ]                     │   OK   │   │
│ To:      [                ]                     ├────────┤   │
│                                                 │ Cancel │   │
│                                                 ├────────┤   │
│                                                 │  Help  │   │
│                                                 └────────┘   │
└──────────────────────────────────────────────────────────────┘
```

PREPARING NEW DISKS

The Disk, Format Disk command formats a floppy diskette in preparation for storing data. Formatting a diskette creates the root directory and deletes any existing information on the disk. Once the Format Disk command is issued, select the diskette drive and capacity from the following dialog box and then press (Enter) or click on OK.

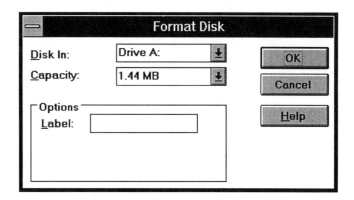

Quick Reference	1. CHOOSE: Disk, Format Disk
Formatting a	2. SELECT: *the desired drive from the Disk In drop-down list box*
Diskette	3. SELECT: *the disk's capacity from the Capacity drop-down list box*
	4. PRESS: (Enter) or CLICK: OK

SUMMARY

This session introduced you to File Manager, the Windows file and directory management program. After a brief explanation of file and disk management basics, the session provided a guided tour of the primary components in the File Manager application window. The most important component is the directory window which provides a graphical depiction of the directory tree and its contents.

Many of the commands and procedures introduced in this session appear in the Command Summary (Table 4.3).

Table 4.3	Command	Description
Command Summary	View, Tree and Directory	Displays the directory tree pane and directory contents pane in the directory window
	View, Tree Only	Displays the directory tree pane only in the directory window
	View, Directory Only	Displays the directory contents pane only in the directory window
	View, Name	Displays the file name and extension for each file in the directory contents pane
	View, All File Details	Displays the file name, extension, size, last modification date and time, and attributes for each file in the directory contents pane
	View, Sort by Name	Sorts files in the directory contents pane by name
	View, Sort by Type	Sorts files in the directory contents pane by the file name extension
	View, Sort by Size	Sorts files in the directory contents pane by size
	View, Sort by Date	Sorts files in the directory contents pane by last modification date
	Window, New Window	Opens a new window that is identical to the active directory window
	Window, Cascade	Layers the open directory windows so that each Title bar is easily viewed and selected
	Window, Tile	Tiles the open directory windows for easy viewing
	File, Copy	Copies selected files from one location to another
	File, Move	Moves selected files from one location to another
	File, Rename	Renames selected files or a directory
	File, Delete (`Delete`)	Deletes selected files or a directory
	File, Create Directory	Creates a new directory

Table 4.3 Continued	Command	Description
	T̲ree, *command*	Expands and collapses the directory tree
	T̲ree, I̲ndicate Expandable Branches	Displays plus and minus signs in the folder icons to represent whether subdirectories are visible
	D̲isk, F̲ormat Disk	Prepares or initializes a new diskette for storage

KEY TERMS

branch In a directory structure, a branch refers to a level in the directory tree; subdirectories branch out from the root directory.

data files Disk files that contain work created or entered using an application software program.

directory structure See *directory tree*.

directory tree The organization of subdirectories on a hard disk or floppy diskette. The root directory appears at the top of the directory tree and subdirectories branch out from the root directory.

directory window A window in the File Manager application window that contains a graphical depiction of the directory tree and its contents.

document files Disk files that contain work created or entered using an application software program recognized by Windows.

drag and drop A feature of File Manager, Microsoft Windows, OS/2, and Macintosh; enables you to copy, move, print, and execute files by dragging a file's icon to a specific location using a mouse.

extension One to three characters added to a file name to aid in file identification. The file name and extension are separated by a period.

file specification   Method of referring to a file or group of files. A file specification consists of the drive letter, directory name, file name, and extension. Wildcard characters (* and ?) are used in a file specification to refer to a general group of files.

parent directory   In a directory structure, the parent directory refers to the directory in the immediately preceding level of the directory tree.

program files   Disk files that contain instructions for the CPU to perform specific tasks or operations.

root directory   In the hierarchy of the directory structure, the first or topmost directory is the root directory; identified by a backslash (\).

Selection cursor   The highlighted bar or frame that is used to select a directory, choose files, and execute commands or programs.

Split bar   The vertical line that separates the directory tree pane from the directory contents pane in the directory window. You can adjust the size of either pane by moving the Split bar.

subdirectories   In the hierarchy of the directory structure, subdirectories appear beneath the root directory. Subdirectories store related program, document, and data files.

wildcard character   The asterisk (*) and question mark (?) are wildcard characters. The asterisk represents a single character, a group of characters, a file name, or an extension in a file specification. The question mark represents a single character in a file specification.

EXERCISES

SHORT ANSWER

1. What are three categories of files that appear on hard disks and floppy diskettes? Define each category.
2. Name the directory where files are stored on a new disk.
3. Explain why subdirectories are important to disk management.
4. Summarize the rules for naming files.
5. Name two methods for selecting a disk drive in the directory window.

6. What information is displayed in the directory contents pane when you choose the <u>V</u>iew, <u>A</u>ll File Details command?
7. How do you move among multiple open windows in the File Manager application window?
8. What are two commands for arranging multiple open windows in the File Manager application window?
9. Explain the drag and drop process for copying a file between drives.
10. What does a + (plus sign) refer to when it appears in a directory folder?

HANDS-ON

(*Note*: In the following exercises, you perform File Manager commands using files located on the Advantage Diskette.)

1. This exercise enables you to practice some of the file management commands that were executed in File Manager during this session.
    a. Ensure that the Advantage Diskette is placed into drive A:.
    b. Open the Main group window and load File Manager.
    c. Display the files from drive A: in the directory window.
    d. Customize the directory window to display only the files.
    e. Sort the files in the directory window by their extensions.
    f. Display the file details for all files in the directory window.
    g. Sort the files by their last modification date.
    h. Sort the files in the directory window by size.
    i. Change the directory window back to the default view with the directory tree pane and the directory contents pane.
    j. Display the filename (including extension) only in the directory contents pane.

2. This exercise gives you practice in copying, deleting, and renaming files on the Advantage Diskette.
    a. With File Manager loaded, ensure that the files on the Advantage Diskette appear in the directory window.
    b. Select the EXPENSES.DBF file in the directory contents pane.
    c. Using the <u>F</u>ile, <u>C</u>opy command, make a backup of the EXPENSES.DBF file to a file called EXPENSES.BAK.
    d. Select the EXPENSES.BAK file.
    e. Rename EXPENSES.BAK to EXPENSES.OLD.
    f. Select all the files appearing in the directory contents pane.
    g. Using <u>F</u>ile, Re<u>n</u>ame, rename all files having the extension OLD to TMP.
    h. Using a mouse, select all the files with the extension TMP.

Session 4 109

   i. Delete all the selected files.

3. This exercise lets you create a directory structure.
   a. With File Manager loaded, ensure that the files on the Advantage Diskette appear in the directory window.
   b. Select the root directory folder in the directory tree pane.
   c. Create the directory tree appearing in Figure 4.8.
   d. Exit File Manager.

Figure 4.8

An example of a directory tree

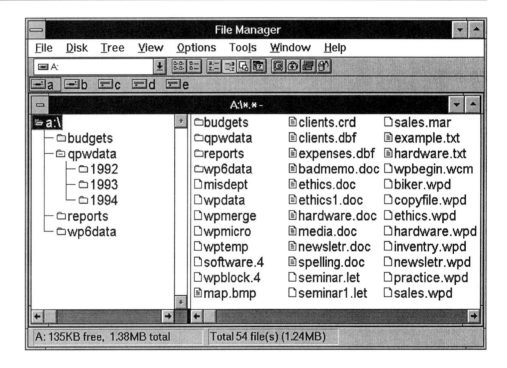

INDEX

SIMPLY WINDOWS

accessory programs, 5, 70
active window, 21, 25
application window, 11, 25
    Control Menu, 12
    Menu Bar, 12, 14
    Minimize and Maximize icons, 13
    Title Bar, 12
arranging windows
    cascade, 19
    tile, 19
ASCII, 71, 76

bitmap graphics, 39, 47
branch, 100, 106

Calculator, 70
Calendar, 70
Cardfile, 70
Clock, 71
color scheme, choosing a, 37
context-sensitive, 45, 47
Control Panel, 36

data files, 83, 106
desktop, 11, 25
dialog box, 15
directory contents pane, 91
    sorting files, 92
    viewing file details, 92
directory structure, 84, 106
directory tree, 84, 106
directory window, 107
disk management, 84
    creating a directory, 99
    formatting a new disk, 104
    removing a directory, 103
    renaming a directory, 104
document files, 83, 107
document window, 11, 13, 25
drag and drop, 95, 107

End mark, 56, 76
exiting Windows, 23
extension, 84, 107

file management, 83
    copying and moving files, 95, 102
    deleting files, 97
File Manager, 4, 85
    directory window, 86, 88
    opening multiple directory windows, 93
    selecting a directory, 101
    selecting a drive, 89
    selecting files, 89
    Selection cursor, 87
    Split bar, 87
    Status bar, 86
file name, 84
file specification, 87, 107
font, 6, 25
footer, 62, 76

games, 21
    Minesweeper, 22
    Solitaire, 21
graphical user interface (GUI), 3, 25
group icons, 25
group windows, 25

header, 62, 76
Help facility, 45
    jump term, 45

icons, 3, 25
insertion point, 56, 76

jump term, 47

Microsoft Windows NT, 6
modem, 71, 77
mouse, 3, 25
moving a window, 18
Multimedia, 55
multimedia applications, 6, 55
multitasking, 7, 25

Notepad, 71

OLE, 7
operating environment, 3
orientation, 43, 47

Paintbrush, 66
    Tool Box icons, 67
parent directory, 107
pattern, choosing a, 39
Print Manager, 5, 43
    choosing a printer, 43
printer drivers, 43, 48
program files, 83, 107
program icons, 26

Program Manager, 4, 31
    creating groups, 33
    deleting groups and program items, 35
    group icons, 11
    group windows, 11
    program icons, 11, 31, 32, 33

queue, 43, 48

root directory, 84, 107

screen saver, 41
Selection area, 59, 77
Selection cursor, 107
sizing a window, 16
Split bar, 107
starting Windows, 9
StartUp group, 33
subdirectories, 107

Task Manager, 5
Terminal, 71
TrueType, 6, 26
typeface, 26
typefaces, 6

wallpaper, choosing a, 39
wildcard character, 107
word processing, 55
word wrap, 55, 77
Write, 55
    creating a document, 56
    exiting Write, 66
    formatting text, 61
    moving around a document, 59
    opening a document, 58
    printing a document, 65
    saving a document, 57
    selecting text, 59
WYSIWYG, 6, 26